75
FSG

ALSO BY IAN FRAZIER

Dating Your Mom
Nobody Better, Better Than Nobody
Great Plains
Family
Coyote v. Acme
It Happened Like This (translator)
On the Rez
The Fish's Eye
Gone to New York
Lamentations of the Father
Travels in Siberia
The Cursing Mommy's Book of Days
Hogs Wild

Cranial Fracking

ery 0ne 0f me? H0w w0uld y0u like
if nine hundred and ninety-nine
ch pe0ple ganged up 0n each 0f
)u? I am n0t afraid t0 call what y0u
ive d0ne—invading my wealthy Zip
0de, burning d0wn all h0u$e$with
)0r $pace 0f m0re than twenty
0u$and $quare feet, and making me
ur "captive"—by it$rightful name,
hich i$cla$$warfare. And yet, f0r all
ur $trength in number$and y0ur
i$guided p0licie$, y0u $till have
)thing t0 write 0n but thi$piece-0f-
nk typewriter. Haven't y0u pe0ple
er heard 0f c0mputer$? 0bvi0u$ly,
ur 0rganizati0n i$a bl0ated, t0p-
avy bureaucracy in which mar-
t f0rce$are n0t all0wed t0 w0rk
0perly. G0d help u$if y0u ever get
ar the c0ntr0l$0f 0ur Dem0cracy!
I am ju$t praying that the "e"
e$n't break 0n thi$crummy thing.
x the rich and $00n we'll all be typ-
g 0n n0n-c0mpetitive techn0l0gy
e thi$, 0r writing with feather$.
) ahead and try to tax me—take
ur be$t $h0t! I'll m0ve my m0ney
the Cayman I$land$$0 fa$t it will
ake y0ur head $pin! "My Cayman$,
$0f thee, $weet land 0f taxe$free,
re c0me my fund$! Land where my
ke$died, land that $ten pace$wide,
ar Cayman I$land$, h0w I tried N0t
pay 0ne dime!" Ye$, it'$a beautiful
untry, the Cayman I$land$, 0w I
·e it—0fi, n0, tfie letter after "g" in
· alpfiabet fia$n0w br0ken al$0! N0w

Cranial Fracking

Ian Frazier

Farrar, Straus and Giroux
New York

Farrar, Straus and Giroux
120 Broadway, New York 10271

"The Roosevelt Outtakes" appears in this volume for the first time. "Enough to Make a Dog Laugh" originally appeared, in slightly different form, in *Outside*, as "How Dogs Laugh with You, Not at You." All other pieces originally appeared, in slightly different form, in *The New Yorker*, with one under a different title: "Italy" as "Never Going to Italy."

Library of Congress Cataloging-in-Publication Data
Names: Frazier, Ian, author.
Title: Cranial fracking / Ian Frazier.
Description: First edition. | New York : Farrar, Straus and
    Giroux, 2021. | Summary: "The great humorist Ian Frazier
    gathers his dispatches from the frontlines of American
    culture"— Provided by publisher.
Identifiers: LCCN 2021014275 | ISBN 9780374603076 (hardcover)
Subjects: LCGFT: Essays.
Classification: LCC PS3556.R363 C73 2021 | DDC 814/.54—dc23
LC record available at https://lccn.loc.gov/2021014275

Our books may be purchased in bulk for promotional, educational, or business use. Please contact your local bookseller or the Macmillan Corporate and Premium Sales Department at 1-800-221-7945, extension 5442, or by email at MacmillanSpecialMarkets@macmillan.com.

www.fsgbooks.com
www.twitter.com/fsgbooks • www.facebook.com/fsgbooks

10 9 8 7 6 5 4 3 2 1

To Mark Singer

Contents

Cranial Fracking

Recap

Keeping a dream journal is also said to promote better recall and to train people to identify signs that indicate they are dreaming—chatting with the deceased, floating cars, talking skeletons.

—*The New York Times*

"I'll have a Rudy's Special, No. 3," the talking skeleton said to the man behind the deli counter. Then he turned to me. "Can you believe those Mets?" the talking skeleton asked. "Have you ever seen such a pathetic choke in your entire life?" The talking skeleton's teeth made a kind of clacking sound as he talked, and his nose holes had some not-yet-decomposed cartilage hanging from them, and a single ant was walking around the inside of one of his eye sockets, counterclockwise.

Normally, I'm a bit shy about talking to people, much less to skeletons fresh from the grave, so I just nodded in agreement. But then I couldn't help adding, "Don't blame Willie Randolph, though!" (I've always liked Willie, since back before he was the Mets' manager, when he was a kid playing for the Yankees.)

The talking skeleton jumped on my remark like it was a slow roller to third. "Absolutely not!" the talking skeleton said, with some heat. "No *way* is that fold-o Willie's fault! But you know who I *do* blame?" He leaned his talking-skeleton head—his skull, technically—close to me.

Talking skeletons always look cheerful, with that grinning skull-mouth they have, but don't let that fool you—they can get really mad. "Rickey Henderson!" the talking skeleton almost yelled, clackingly. "I blame Rickey Henderson!" Then the skeleton went on about what a dumb idea it was for the Mets to hire Henderson as a base-running coach, especially after the incident back in '99, when he played cards in the clubhouse, and so on.

At this point, I was starting to wonder how a talking skeleton was going to eat a Rudy's Special, No. 3, anyway. It's delicious, but it's like a chicken parmesan patty on a roll, with melted cheese and sauce on top. I could imagine long ropes of melted cheese getting stuck on the talking skeleton's many sharp surfaces and creating quite a mess. But, hey, he wants a No. 3, that's his business.

Now the talking skeleton was leaving. At the door, he turned and intoned, skeleton-like, "It was the worst collapse in the entire history of organized baseball!" Then he clattered out.

Quite honestly, I had begun to think I was dreaming.

Somehow, I didn't feel hungry enough for a No. 3, so I just ordered a liverwurst on rye with lettuce and mustard, and a Diet Coke. Just then, my cell phone started vibrating in my pocket. I took it out and saw that the call was from Jawaharlal Nehru, the late prime minister of India, calling from Mumbai. Better take that call.

"Jawaharlal, buddy," I said, fumbling for the bills to pay for my sandwich. "How goes it? Did you see the game?"

Just then, the talking skeleton came back in. "Is that Nehru?" he asked. "Let me talk to him when you're done."

I nodded my head and held up one finger, indicating that he could have the phone in a minute.

". . . most certainly did see the game," Nehru was saying. "I watched all but the ninth inning on the small-screen TV in my invisible floating limousine." Nehru, in case you've forgotten, was elected president of the Indian National Congress six times, and became India's prime minister in 1947, helping the country through its difficult early years of independence while scouting for the old Milwaukee Braves. He proceeded to give me, and then the talking skeleton, an earful about the failures of the Mets' front office, coming down particularly hard on the assistant general manager, Tony Bernazard, whom he accused of undercutting Willie every chance he (Bernazard) got.

A vague sense of disquiet began to steal over me. What, I wondered, could the Mets have done differently last season? And why was I wearing only underpants? True, the weather had been unusually warm for October, and anyone as upset as I had been about the Mets' catastrophic disgrace could hardly be expected to pay much attention to clothes. Still, I wished that I had thought to bring a robe or a towel along, and that Lastings Milledge had run out one or two more ground balls. To add to that, the entire delicatessen and all the people in it had begun to plummet through space at an alarming rate, going down in a giant vortex-whirlpool thing that was kind of a dark green at the outer edges and became a blinding white the closer you got to the center, making it even harder to concentrate.

The answer, I think, is training. Each of us has a job to

do. The Mets have to go back to good, hard, solid, fundamental baseball and focus on doing the little things right. That means not trying to steal third with two men out, Mr. José Reyes! And, as for me, I have got to start being more conscientious about my dream journal. I've been letting that slide, I admit. With a little discipline and training and the help of my journal, I'll be able to recognize the important signs. Talking skeleton equals dream. Chatting with the dead: dream. Floating cars (or any other normally earthbound vehicle): dream. Mets losing first place to the Phillies on the last day of the season: reality. Once I hone those reactions until they're second nature so that I don't even have to think about them, I'll be better off.

By the Foot

I feel sorry for people who still think of their places in terms of square feet. My partner, Scott, and I recently purchased Wyoming, which we are in the process of having renovated, and, yes, I do know the square footage (something like two trillion seven hundred and thirty billion square feet, give or take). But that's just not a very practical type of measurement when we're dealing with all the plumbers and contractors and security staff and reporters and other non-wealthy service personnel we have to give instructions to. Nowadays, everybody involved in redoing substantial properties like ours uses Global Transverse Mercator Units (GTMUs), which you get off a satellite feed. GTMUs, we've found, are much more accurate for detail work like wainscoting, and are able to deal with vast alkali flats and so on, too.

Basically, we are looking at this purchase as a teardown. There's really not a lot here you'd want to keep, except one or two of the Wind River Mountains and some old 1920s Park Service structures in Yellowstone. Scott and I bought for the location—it's convenient to anywhere, really, if you think about it—and for the simplicity of line. We wanted someplace rectangular, a much easier configuration from a design point of view, and we won't have to fuss with panhandles and changeable riverine property lines where we're going to get into disputes with the landowner next door. Spare us the headaches, please! We've had plenty already, with the former occupants (thank heavens they're gone) and all the junk they left behind—the old broken-down pickup trucks, houses, eyesore water towers, uranium mines, the University of Wyoming, Yellowtail Dam, Casper. I'm a thrower-outer. I believe we must first clear everything away, then see what we've got. Scott is more sentimental. He thinks we should leave the North Platte River, for example, and work around it. I haven't said yes or no. I'm secretly hoping he changes his mind.

In fact, I get a little crazy when I think about it. I should block this question from my consciousness entirely. The North Platte River is the most ridiculous . . . It's literally "a mile wide and an inch deep." That's literally true. There are these small trickles of water running here and there, kind of a brownish sand stretching in all directions, a few cow footprints, weird little bushes, a rusty car axle sticking up out of the brownish sand. Why would you ever want to hang on to something like that?

I know that he's not really serious. I know this is just a ploy to get back at me for insisting on separate bathrooms and then taking first pick. For mine, I chose Johnson and Sheridan Counties, and he's in a silent rage because his bathroom will be a couple of counties that are a short drive down the interstate, that's all. Nothing, nothing puts a strain on a relationship like redoing a home.

Forgive me if I've neglected to introduce myself. My name is on the card that you were given earlier. You'll note that both my first and last names are blacked out; feel free to use a thick black line when referring to either of them. Scott, of course, is a pseudonym, for personal reasons not disclosed. The so-called Scott and I request that all media coverage refrain from any mention of us in connection with the recently purchased real estate described above. This is a privacy issue and goes to the heart of us not wanting you to know. The electrified double fencing along the border of South Dakota and the other still existing neighbor states makes the intended point as well, we trust.

Will our new digs be costly to heat in the winter and air-condition in the summer? Yes, absolutely. What about problems of sewage and toxic runoff? That will all go to Colorado. Who will handle waste disposal? You, the taxpayer. What about trespassers inadvertently crossing our property lines? Of course, we expect all transcontinental passenger and military flights to detour around our yard and not cut across. That's just common courtesy. All pilots, I think, should be aware that when they approach certain latitudinal and longitudinal coordinates they are entering a private residence. A little consideration here, please.

I guess there's not much more you need to know. As I revisit some of my earlier statements having to do with our personality conflicts involving the North Platte River and so on, I want all that taken out. Internal matters of that kind are outside the bounds of what needs to be talked about here. We have really a lot of money—that is the essential point, so let's stick to just describing that. "A lot" doesn't even convey it, because people will think in ordinary terms of "a lot," which is misleading. The total (if I even knew it) is like a lot, a lot, a lot, times even a huge amount more than that. It's almost frustrating not to be able to get this across.

Sometimes I use the living room metaphor. Your living room—and it doesn't matter who "you" are, because "you" could be anybody, except for a handful of people like me— the living room you are most familiar with, in your own house, is (to me) inconceivably small, of course.

All right. Now imagine the people whom I feel sorry for, mentioned previously, stuck in the old "square feet" paradigm; imagine, further, that I run into them in Davos or somewhere, and they start boring me with talk about their fabulous "walk-in" closets, the ones that are the size of your living room. Do you see? Isn't it clear that this would drive me and anyone close to me absolutely insane? When all the closets in our new place will be constructed to provide fly-through access for helicopters or bush aircraft? Can you see how hard it is for me to keep pretending that we're talking about the same thing?

I believe you do know what I mean. Yes—I sense that you do understand me, and in a very deep and visceral way. Listen, I like your style. Though you're a member of the media, you comport yourself in a manner that is pleasing to me. I'll even go one better—I want to hire you to come and work for my company, or whatever it is that I do. Tell me what they're paying you and I'll third it.

I'm sorry, I must've misheard you. "No"? Did I hear "no"? Who the hell do you think you are? Why, I'll make sure you never work in this quadrant of the universe again. Oh, so now you want to reconsider my offer, do you? Lucky for you I'm a forgiving person. Very well. You start tomorrow morning. I'll expect you in my office at 6:45—that's down the hall, around the buttes, first sky-high triumphal archway on your right. Knock twice and leave your shoes on the Divide.

A. S. A. P.

Dear Sir or Madam:

Recently, your name was suggested to the Prize Committee of the Milo and Angeline Bupkas Foundation as a person of unusual or extraordinary merit in the arts who might benefit from a letter in the mail such as this one. Only a small number of men and women, all of them listed in their fields, will receive this mailing honor. We expect you to act upon it with dispatch and full consideration.

What we are about to say is completely confidential. Please do not mention to anybody that you received this letter. Do not read it where anybody can see.

About three weeks ago, the Bupkas Prize Committee was given the name of a certain individual said to be well qualified as someone to recommend someone to receive a prestigious Bupkas Prize. After some inquiries, we have determined that this recommending individual is personally known to you. We are asking whether you, in your careful opinion, would recommend this person to recommend somebody to us, or not.

As you yourself are known to the Prize Committee only by hearsay, we ask that you also submit references from six colleagues who can vouch for your reliability in dealing with this matter. All documents sent to the Prize Committee are due by the first of the month. Those which arrive after the deadline are considered late, and go straight into the wastepaper basket, and are then destroyed.

As you may be aware, the Milo and Angeline Bupkas Foundation was established by Milo Bupkas in memory of his late wife, Angeline. Recalling his wife's lifelong fondness for poetry readings that were open to the public at no cost, he commemorated her enthusiasm in a foundation endowed with a Bupkas start-up donation to cover operating expenses and prize awards. Since then, the Bupkas Foundation has been involved with a number of exciting projects, in fulfillment of its motto, "Giving Bupkas to the Arts Every Day."

None of the above information need immediately concern you, however, so keep it under your hat. When you have read this letter and fully complied with its instructions, please burn it or forward it to a reputable shredding company. Then forget about it completely—that is, if you value the safety of your family. Remember that literally thousands of dollars of arts funding may be involved.

In recommending the aforementioned person who will be doing the actual candidate recommendation, we hope you will address the following concerns: First, any person who recommends somebody must be a resident. Ignoring this criterion will invalidate his or her application. Second, to participate, neither the recommender nor the candidate may be the recipient of any other prize, grant, honorarium, stipend, bank-to-bank wire transfer, income tax refund, Social Security or WIC/AFDC payment, veteran's benefit, or postal remittance of any kind. Please do not submit the individuals themselves.

In your own assistant's words, state why the recommender in question deserves to be given this demanding responsibility. Your comments may take the form of a standard expository letter, confessional essay, or choreo-poem. All submissions must be signed, double-spaced, typed legibly, and encrypted in Linear B cuneiform. Minimum length is forty pages. People sometimes ask if they are allowed to smoke. The answer, of course, is no.

After having completed this document and scanned it for viruses, you will be asked to submit to a full body cavity search and then flown to a secure location overseas. These measures are only precautionary, to ensure that you do not chatter drunkenly at a faculty cocktail party and let something slip. On our word as arts administrators, we assure you that what we are doing in this regard is absolutely necessary. If you were even unintentionally to reveal that you were recommending somebody to choose somebody to be a candidate for the prized Bupkas Prize, and that person passed along to a protégé that he or she might be nominated for a Bupkas, and that second person, the potential nominee, went to the first person's (the nominator's) house with a bunch of hot friends, and they all offered to perform certain services or acts for that nominating person in return for preference, and a bystander with a handheld video camera happened to be present at the time, and he or she made videos of the goings-on, and those videos were posted on the internet, obviously that could result in serious harm.

Before reading beyond this point, please have yourself bonded. From here to the end of this letter, all information is "eyes only" and must go no farther than these four walls.

From the moment you began reading this letter, you have been under surveillance. Please do not look up or betray any alarm. You are already involved in this more deeply than you know. Our only wish at this point is to protect you, so pay close attention to what we are about to say. Milo Bupkas is a complete madman. We are putting our own lives in danger by telling you this, but it's true. Here is how the plan will go down: You will send in your assessment of the person who is to do the recommendation. He or she will nominate a candidate, who will file the necessary paperwork. Then, regardless of the outcome, all three of you will be put on mailing lists—both regular and email. Later on, these lists will be sold in a way that is meant to appear accidental. The Bupkas Foundation's "mechanics" are highly skilled at that.

If you want to walk out of this, do exactly as we instruct you now. Finish reading this letter and casually toss it back on your desk. Stand up and stretch and yawn. Walk over to the cabinet and take your wallet, passport, and keys. Remove five hundred thousand in euros from the bottom drawer and put it in a shopping bag. Unfortunately, there will be no time to kiss your spouse goodbye. Walk slowly from the house until you come to a brightly lit public place. Then take off running as fast as you can, screaming at the top of your lungs. Do not stop until you reach the Mexican or Canadian border. We have never been more serious in our lives, and we thank you for your prompt attention.

Mi Chiamo Stan

He was a hardworking farm boy. She was an Italian supermodel. He knew he would have just one chance to impress her.

—Advertisement for language-learning software program

LESSON 1—Beginning conversation; basic nouns and verbs. Memorize the following vocabulary:

Hello!—*Ciao!*
name—*nome*
telephone number—*numero di telefono*
to live—*vivere*
Quad Cities—*Città "Quad"*
Valentino—*Valentino*
ag school—*scuola agraria*
to be—*essere*
stock-tank de-icer—*macchina che toglie il ghiaccio dal serbatoio dell'abbeveratoio*
Fall Fashion Week—*Settimana della Moda dell'Autunno*

Sample sentences. Practice saying these out loud:

Hello! May I have your name and telephone number?
Ciao! Potrei avere il suo nome ed il suo numero di telefono?

My name is Stan, which is a nickname for Stancil.
Mi chiamo Stan, che è il diminutivo di Stancil.

I live on a farm near the Quad Cities.
Vivo in una fattoria vicino alle Città "Quad."

They are Moline, Rock Island, Davenport, and Bettendorf.
Sono Moline, Rock Island, Davenport, e Bettendorf.

Not many people know what the Quad Cities are.
Non molte persone sanno cosa sono le Città "Quad."

East Moline is technically one of the Quad Cities also, but it's usually left out, because that would make five.
Tecnicamente, East Moline è una delle Città "Quad," ma di solito si omette perché sennò sarebbero cinque.

Who is your favorite Italian fashion designer?
Chi è il suo stilista italiano preferito?

Personally, I have been a fan of Valentino ever since ag school.
Personalmente, sono stato un ammiratore di Valentino fin dalla scuola agraria.

During Milan's Fall Fashion Week, in which hotel will you be staying?
Durante la Settimana della Moda dell'Autunno di Milano, in quale hotel starà?

Could you please give me directions how to get to that hotel from western Illinois?

Per favore, mi potrebbe indicare la strada per quell'hotel partendo dall'Illinois occidentale?

Now I must repair the stock-tank de-icer in our back pasture.

Ora devo riparare la macchina che toglie il ghiaccio dal serbatoio dell'abbeveratoio, che sta nel pascolo.

It is a piece of junk, and has once again broken down.

È un relitto, e si è rotto ancora una volta.

Well, goodbye, and have a good day, okay?

Arrivederci, e buona giornata, okay?

LESSON 3—Regular verbs. Familiarize yourself with the conjugation of the verb "to milk" (*mungere*):

I milk *io mungo*
you (s.) milk *tu mungi*
he/she milks *lui/lei munge*
we milk *noi mungiamo*
you (pl.) milk *voi mungete*
they milk *loro mungono*
Milk! (imp.) *Mungi!* (s.)
   Mungete! (pl.)

Many other verbs—to water (*innaffiare*), to hay (*falciare il fieno*), to pose (*posare*), to mow (*mietere*), to pleat (*pieghettare*), to manure (*concimare*), to accessorize (*dotare di accessori*), to sashay (*ancheggiare*), to diet (*fare la dieta*), to apply bag balm (*applicare balsalmo per mammelle*), and to hiss (*fischiare*)—take more or less the same endings, so it will be useful to learn them all.

LESSON 7—At the Fuel Co-op.

Now you are ready to make simple purchases and discuss everyday topics with people on the street. Repeat this typical conversation alone or with a partner until it comes naturally to you:

Good afternoon, Owney. I would like to buy two tanks of propane.
Buon pomeriggio, Owney. Vorrei comprare due serbatoi di propano, per favore.

I said, "I would like to buy some propane!"
Ho detto, "Vorrei comprare del propano!"

Of course you can't understand me. That is because I am talking in Italian.
Certo lei non può capirmi. Sarà perché sto parlando in italiano.

Laugh if you wish, Owney, but someday I will be having sex with a beautiful Italian supermodel in Milan, Italy, while you are still here sweeping fertilizer pellets off the floor.
Rida se vuole, Owney, ma un giorno farò sesso con una

top model italiana a Milano, Italia, mentre lei sarà qui a spazzare via le palline di fertilizzante.

Well, goodbye, Owney. I will buy my propane another day.

Arrivederci, Owney. Comprerò il propano un altro giorno.

LESSON 13—Verbs of motion. Italian verbs of motion use different forms depending on their contexts, as the following examples demonstrate:

to drive (in a vehicle)—*guidare*
to ride—*farsi dare un passaggio*
to walk—*camminare*
Example: If you will not drive me to the bus station, Mom, I will ride with the mailman, or walk.

Mamma, se non mi porti alla stazione degli autobus, mi farò dare un passaggio dal postino, o camminerò.

to run—*correre*
to fall—*cadere*
to board—*imbarcarsi*
Example: I ran down the concourse, fell over somebody's suitcase, and boarded my flight to Milan just in time.

Correvo lungo l'atrio, e sono caduto sulla valigia di qualcuno, ma poi mi sono imbarcato per Milano giusto in tempo.

to fly—*volare*
to hurl—*lanciare*

Example: I don't like to fly. I might hurl.

Non amo volare. Potrei lanciare.

LESSON 18—At the police station.

Often, foreigners who can speak Italian have difficulty understanding native speakers when they talk quickly, use idioms, or do not pause for response. Listen to the following common sentences in the audio portion of the lesson and replay them as often as you need to.

May I see your passport, please?
Potrei vedere il suo passaporto, per favore?

I must ask you to come with me.
Devo chiederle di venire con me.

Spread your arms and place your hands against the wall.
Stenda le braccia e collochi le mani contro il muro.

Are you aware that stalking a supermodel without her consent is a violation of Italian law?
Lei è consapevole che infastidire una top model senza il suo consenso è una violazione della legge italiana?

This pocket dictionary of Italian prison slang may be useful to you.
Questo dizionario tascabile di gergo carcerario italiano le potrebbe essere utile.

Please surrender your chewing tobacco to the desk clerk. It will be returned to you upon your release.

Per favore depositi il suo tabacco da masticare all'impie-gato. Le sarà restituito quando sarà rilasciato.

LESSON 25—Review and summary.

Congratulations on completing this introductory course in spoken Italian! Now that you have put in all the required work, you may be interested to know that most of the people you will meet in Italy probably speak English already. Diplomats, tour guides, stylists, supermodels, and so on may be relied on to have a good command of our language. In that regard, you have largely wasted your time.

Just because they speak English, however, does not mean these folks are a breeze to understand. Quite the contrary! Often, their speech is heavily accented and their phrasing and word use are so eccentric that you must pay close attention in order to get their meaning. Practice your comprehension skills by listening to the passage on the audio as you follow along below:

"Ah, Stancil, I am so *fortunata* that you came into my life! At first, true, I did not—*come si dice*—realize what a blessing you were for me. And, true, I had you jailed in prison, but later I changed my thoughts, and paid your bail money, so we could be together now and always. Your love rescued me from the cruel fates of catwalk model, such as attending parties and enjoying cocaine and earning many, many *milioni* every year or even every month—but at such a cost! My unnatural thinness, so unwelcome for me, so *malsana*, when my bust measurement is in fact fuller than is suggested in this industry! Always my dream has been to meet a young American with a dairy-cow-and-feeder-pig operation somewhere in the valley of the Des Plaines River of Illinois, to where we will now go *immediatamente* so we can be married and have many children, and I will join the local 4-H advisers' group to give me something to do when I am not cooking gourmet Italian dinners for you and satisfying you matrimonially!"

Pinch yourself to test your comprehension.

Lines on the Poet's Turning Forty

I.
And so, at last, I am turning forty,
In just a couple of days.
The big four-oh.
Yes, that is soon to be my age.
(And not fifty-eight. No way. That Wikipedia is a bunch of
   liars.)
Nope, not any other age, just forty.
What other age could someone born in 1969 (and not 1951)
Possibly be?
(And please do not listen to my ex-wife, that sad, bitter
   woman in her late fifties.)
What does it feel like, old bones?
Yes, I have lost a step or two in the hundred-meter dash.
I accept these changes.
But if a guy says in a published poem that he is forty,
As I am doing here,
It's obvious that must be the age that he is,
Officially.

II.
Cattail down blows from the swamp like smoke,
Ice bares its teeth on the surface of the mud puddles.
It is fall—but not for me in any metaphorical sense,

Because forty, while not technically all that young, is
    hardly like "the autumn of life" or anything;
And also because Natalie Portman, the famous actress,
Is in love with me. And why not?
After all, there is not that much difference, age-wise,
Between a person who I guess is in her mid-to-late twenties
And a person who is only just turning forty,
I.e., me.

III.

You walk across the room carrying a bouquet of phlox in
    your hand
("You" being Natalie Portman, the famous actress)
As a present for me on my upcoming fortieth birthday.
Come sit beside me, my dear,
And I will tell you about my previous thirty-nine,
Except for the year when I was in sixth grade,
Which is a total blank.
I do remember fifth grade, when we had Mrs. Erwin,
And seventh grade, when we moved to the new junior high
    building;
But when I try to remember sixth—nothing.
Let us not mourn what is lost.
Sixth grade was probably not that great.
Now, and on into the serious years that lie ahead,
You and I will have each other.

IV.

An alert reader may point out
That we did not move to the new junior high building
    during the 1981–82 school year

(As would fit with my being in seventh grade and having
        been born in 1969)
But eighteen years earlier, in the school year of 1963–64.
This is baloney!
Whoever says such statements is wrong.
I think that when it comes to the details of my own life
My own word should be trusted over that of some random
        reader,
Thank you!

V.

Unfortunately, because of this business
About when we did or didn't move to the new junior high
        building,
Natalie Portman's suspicions somehow were raised,
And she had a completely unnecessary "background
        check" run on me,
And then left me for Thane Goltz,
Who is hot right now.

VI.

This poem is becoming a disaster.
It happens sometimes—
I get into a poem, and the thing goes haywire,
And I don't know how to get out.
According to some nitpicker at the Ohio Department of
        Education,
Mrs. Roberta Erwin retired and left teaching entirely in
        1967,
Two years before my birth.
Thus, the argument goes,

She could not have taught me fifth grade,
As I claimed in Canto III.

VII.
Look, I am turning forty, all right?
Let's just leave it at that.
Critics and people in the media who would ruin a
      celebration with this kind of "gotcha" behavior make
      me sick.
If you still doubt me,
Please be assured that this publication has a rigorous policy
      of fact-checking,
And all the information in this poem has been checked,
And directly verified by me.

VIII.
Well, it's going to be great being forty.
I am looking forward to it.
There are plenty of other beautiful actresses around;
I may also try out for the forty-and-over division
On the National Professional Rodeo Association tour.
Recently someone asked me if I remembered when the
      name
Of Idlewild Airport in New York City
Was changed to JFK International.
"Of course not," I replied.
"That was long before my time.
Back then I had not even been born."

The Temperature of Hell: A Colloquium

According to the best scientific data currently available, both the average and the mean temperatures of Hell have risen 3.8 degrees since 1955. Although an increase of this size may seem insignificant, especially to those not spending eternity there, the reality of the situation is quite different when experienced in concrete terms. For example, occupants of Hell who in 1955 were standing night and day in boiling pitch up to their knees report that, owing to the expansion of pitch at higher temperatures, they now must endure the torment all the way up to mid-thigh, or even higher, during Hell's warmer seasons. Condemned souls who have to lie on their backs chained to a flat rock while a white-hot sheet of iron is lowered to within inches of their faces have stated that the rise in Hell's ambient temperature now makes the iron seem much closer to their faces than it actually is.

Former vice president Al Gore, who was among the first to raise concerns about this problem, recently convened an interdisciplinary gathering to discuss some of Hell's climate issues and how we might begin to address them. To encourage the widest possible range of views, Mr. Gore invited a mixture of climate experts, satanic functionaries, representatives of industry, people from the faith community, average citizens, advocates for the aged, and a large number of the souls of the damned who are dealing with these changes on a daily basis. Owing to travel restrictions on some of the participants, the convocation took place deep in a smoldering, sulfurous Hell-mouth below a subbasement in the Sony Building. The following is an edited transcript:

MR. GORE: Thank you all for coming today—is that rotten egg smell bothering anybody? We're working on getting some fans to ventilate that out of here—and I'd like to start right in with a question for those of you who have temporarily ascended from the innermost bowels of Hades. You know what it's like down there, while many of us still don't. First off, I think we'd all like to know: How hot is it?

MR. MAGUS: Thank you, Mr. Gore, for convening this distinguished assembly, and I'm honored you invited me. My name is Simon Magus and I am, or was, a Samaritan sorcerer of the first century consigned to everlasting perdition for the sin of simony, the selling of church offices or preferments (a sin actually named after me). I've been in Hell for going on two millennia now, and, to be honest with you, I haven't noticed that much of a difference. I'm told it's hotter lately, and I guess I'll take your word for it. But where I am, down in the Third Chasm, it's incredible. I mean, flames fall on our bare feet constantly, the rock our bodies are stuck in is practically on fire—it's Hell, basically, so it's very, very hot already. I just worry that we might be making a big deal out of nothing here.

MS. BIELUSKA: Can I respond to that?

MR. GORE: Please, go ahead.

MS. BIELUSKA: Mr. Gore, I am the shade of Amber Catherine Bieluska, of Lakewood, Ohio, and I would like to disagree strongly with the statement that has just been made. I am in Hell for a lot of minor things, the biggest one being that I never paid the sixties band that played at my third wedding, and I'm supposed to be enduring only mild agony in First Circle Plus, which is as high in Hell as you can go, and my own personal suffering and atonement have gotten so much worse just in the past few years. Where I'm at, it's always been more stuffy than really *hot* hot, but recently it's become so damp and humid, and, with the incoming spirit traffic and all the particle pollution from that, I feel my own punishment, which was totally unfair to begin with, has been made much more horrible through no fault of my own.

MR. GORE: Thank you, Ms. Bieluska and Mr. Magus, and we'll be coming back to you shortly, but now I'd like to turn to one of the country's leading authorities on terrestrial and infernal climates, Dr. James Hansen, of NASA's Goddard Institute for Space Studies. Dr. Hansen, tell us, are we "making a big deal out of nothing"?

DR. HANSEN: Thank you, Mr. Vice President, and I extend greetings to all you folks, former folks, and Satan-serving fiends who have taken the time to attend this vitally important event. I wish I could say we *were* making too much of Hell's growing problems, but I'm afraid the news in that area is very grim indeed. As you may know, more human beings now occupy our planet than have occupied it at any other time in all of history or prehistory—some seven billion souls, and counting—and when these people die, as they're all going to do, we can anticipate that all but .0001 percent of them will not be going to Heaven. Granted, a lot of these will stop at Purgatory, but the rest will descend directly to Hell. We expect that the sudden influx of souls will put a huge strain on Hell's carrying capacity and make large regions of it virtually uninhabitable.

Now, we are accustomed to thinking of the basic affliction of Hell as the burning brimstone—and, yes, brimstone *is* a significant part of the package, with its horrible odor and disgusting yellow color and the way it sticks to the skin and so on. But brimstone is essentially just sulfur, a rather expensive commodity when compared with, say, coal. And the fact is that owing to cost considerations, low-grade soft coal—so-called dirty coal—is currently providing more than 93 percent of the energy for the fires of Hell. At the rate of growth we're seeing now, consumption of that amount of coal for all eternity is simply unsustainable. As you know, I have recently been involved in an international committee looking into Hell's long-term energy picture, and we have recommended that Hell convert as soon as possible from a coal-based soul-scourging system to one that relies on clean-burning, plentiful, and inexpensive natural gas. Now, I am aware that this idea has not been popular among the dark powers and principalities, but—

(Here the tape of the proceedings is interrupted by blasts of deafening static from the electromagnetic emanations of the demons, tempters, subtempters, satyrs, and gargoyles who begin to burst through interstices in the Hell-mouth's crusted floor, flying redly past the speaker's dais and among the participants looking on from folding chairs. An unholy

discord and din, with howling and gnashing of teeth un-transcribable. Now a molten sinkhole appears and advances gurgling until it reaches Mr. Gore and sucks him from view.)

"Hello? Hello? . . . Is this thing on? . . . Hello, this is Al Gore, and I'm fine, my pant cuffs are singed and the bottoms of my shoes are smoking a little, but I want to emphasize that I am okay. I am going to continue to talk into this lavalier microphone clipped to my shirt collar in the hope that those of you up top can still hear me. What has happened is that I seem to have slid down a chute type of deal into the vestibule of Hell itself. It's uncomfortably warm here, no question about that, and there are big red neon signs saying YOU ARE IN HELL—GET USED TO IT!, and now I see a robed spirit figure walking toward me and— Hey, wait a minute! Is that . . . is that *Mickey Mantle?*"

"Welcome to Hell, Mr. Vice President, and, yes, you are correct, I am the spiritual remnant of what used to be Mickey Mantle—baseball legend and executive. I have been consigned to this place not for anything I did on the diamond but for some of my off-the-field antics, as detailed in such books as *Ball Four,* by Jim Bouton, and Billy Martin's *Number 1.* If those books had not been written, my sins probably would have escaped notice—but, hey, I'm not complaining. So far I've been enjoying my assignment as Hell's official greeter, and I'd love to take you on a look around. May I?"

"Lead away, Mick!"

"All right, Mr. Vice President—watch your head as we go down this hot lava staircase here, and over on your *zzzt* left you can see the *zzzt* where teachers who were *zzzt* mean to *zzzt* in elementary sch_zzzt_ must suffer *zzzt zzzt zzzzzzzzzzzt . . .*"

(At this point, Mr. Gore descended beyond the coverage area and began to break up. The colloquium adjourned for a ninety-minute lunch, after which the transcript resumes.)

SATAN HIMSELF: Could everybody please take their seats? Surrender your souls to me and worship and obey me? Thank you. I'm told that Sony will need this space back by 5:00 p.m., and there's still a lot left on the agenda, so we have to move along. Some of you might not recognize me without the big cape and the collar that goes all the way up to my horns, and my tail is tucked into my right pant leg, but I'm Beelzebub, Mephistopheles, Abaddon, Baal, Old Nick, Mr. Blackburn, Randi Weingarten, or whatever name I'm being given these days. Mr. Gore has thoughtfully suggested that while he's finishing his tour I rise from my foul throne at the absolute lowest depths of perfidy and corruption to address you about the troubling situation we're facing in Hell today.

Right now in Hell we are hurting. That's the single most important takeaway I would like you to get from what I have to say to you this afternoon: we are hurting. Hell is being pressed to and beyond its limits to such an extent that we are having trouble simply performing our jobs. Every day, I must make hard choices from among an inadequate supply of options. People in the land of the living are constantly requesting that this or that other person "rot in Hell," and we've always tried to accommodate that, and as a result we have literally tens of billions of individuals—tier after tier after *tier* of them—sitting there rotting, and we have had to put in new tiers and still they are all over the place. And is anybody besides us giving any thought to maintenance? To the necessary monitoring of the rot? To staffing? I'm a detail-oriented type, I'm actually *in* the details, and recently that's been where I'm falling down, and it's impacting my most important attribute, which is my pride. I like my helper devils to have the best titanium pitchforks, and that's been impossible for us under current conditions, so they've been having to just sort of poke the wretched sinners with their long and pointy fingernails. That's only one example.

Because of ongoing constraints, I am sorry to say, the operation of Hell is no longer even close to what it should be, and important areas of quality are being degraded. I hate with my most ancient and implacable hatred of all that is good to have to say this, but unfortunately it's true. So, for me, the whole increase-in-temperature thing, while important, is pretty far down on my list of concerns. I can stand at the exact center of the sun, temperature twenty-eight million degrees Fahrenheit, and it's like a summer breeze to me. Far as I'm concerned, warming is not the problem; it's the overall decline in Hell's capabilities. Right now, with the resources we're being given, we are not punishing souls for their specific transgressions anymore, we're just warehousing them. And that's a shame.

So when you look at your kids asleep in their beds after you return to your homes this evening, I want you to ask yourselves, "What kind of Hell am I leaving for them, and for my grandchildren?" Once we've all thought about that, maybe we can set aside personal concerns and begin to act in the larger interest of Hell. But now I am being informed that my time is up. Do you know who you're talking to? Do you have any *idea* who you are talking to? May I do my laugh before I go?

Fanshawe

Fanshawe had just the one name. He didn't mind this, having come from a long line of single-name Fanshawes. Fanshawe's father, also, was Fanshawe—just Fanshawe— while his mother, née Richardson, had never been known by any name but that until she married Fanshawe's father, whereupon she became (somewhat less simply) Fanshawe-Richardson. The cumbersomeness of such a string of syllables finally proving too much for her, she shortened this formulation to Fanshawe-, and then quietly dropped the hyphen some years afterward. The Fanshawes' union produced four children—Fanshawe, a younger brother, and two older sisters. Each, of course, was christened Fanshawe. The family had been in New England for generations and did not approve of excessive fuss. Having six people in the same house all called Fanshawe, without further designation or perhaps a number system to distinguish one from another, made for obvious complications, but we needn't let that trouble us here, because I think both the reader and I know which Fanshawe I mean, namely, the Fanshawe in the first sentence, whom I was originally referring to, and whom this story is about.

When the time came for Fanshawe to marry, he surprised his friends and family by choosing a foreign student from Seville, Spain, who had about eleven names—Maria Conchita Something Something DiBiasio y Cosmo Something, and so on. I never met this wife, and so am not in a position to judge her. The marriage soon ended in divorce. For the rest of his twenties and into his early thirties, Fanshawe "played the field," as we used to say. In college, Fanshawe's social set had included an unusual number of men—Neuman, Farrel, Fogel, Harrison, Fegley, Carson, Foster, Ferguson, Sapers, Miles, Northon, Winslow—who were mononomes like himself. Aside from this evident preference, Fanshawe could in no way have been described as a snob. But, when he determined to marry for a second time, he seemed almost perversely to delight in informing his intimates that his new bride possessed no name at all.

The wedding ceremony was of the sort in which the couple have written their own vows and a compliant reverend presides. The bride had announced that she would be keeping her own name, or lack of one, so the expected difficulties this presented in the proceedings were gotten around by saying "[bride's name here]" whenever she had to be referred to. "I, [bride's name here], do take you, Fanshawe, to be my lawfully wedded husband," and so on. Well, it was awkward, and more than faintly ridiculous, but none of us who attended these odd nuptials raised an eyebrow. All of us were old enough by now to have learned that what goes on between two people in a marriage can never be accurately gauged from the outside.

Looking back, I can't say exactly when it was that things started to go to pieces for Fanshawe. His marriage certainly didn't help matters any. From the punctiliousness with which he spoke of, and insisted others speak of, his new bride, you might have thought she was the ineffable, unnameable divinity Herself. Whenever you asked after the wife, you had to sort of slur the word, or swallow it, as in "How's your *w, w*, you know, your *w*—?"

In correspondence, Fanshawe wouldn't even spell it out, but used ampersands for the vowels. Then, in the middle of all this, as if demoralized by the mounting confusion, Fanshawe's parents both died. First Fanshawe, the father, keeled over deader than a Portuguese mackerel on the paddle tennis court one afternoon, only to be followed in quick succession by Fanshawe, Fanshawe's mother, who pitched headfirst from a birding tower on the East Coast flyway near Cape May. An autopsy later revealed that she had died of plaid.

Their deaths left Fanshawe absolutely bereft—and by Fanshawe I mean, of course, the person I've been focusing on from the beginning, and none of the other Fanshawes, though I intend them no disrespect. Obviously, they have a right to be called whatever they want. As the chronicler of these events, however, I would like to register my distinct annoyance at having to write about so many people of the same name. For at this point (the senior Fanshawes having died intestate) I must describe several lawsuits wherein Fanshawe, the elder of the sisters, sued Fanshawe, the brother, while Fanshawe, the younger sister, sued all three of her Fanshawe siblings, including Fanshawe. (And by this last Fanshawe I am of course indicating, etc., etc.) In passing, I can only warn other authors that if they are ever tempted to write about a stylish main character who possesses just a single name, they run a serious risk of falling into exactly the sort of tangle I find myself in here.

There turned out to be a lot of one-name Fanshawes, all right? I guess I did fail to anticipate that. And I'll be up-front with you—I honestly don't care in the slightest about any of the others except as they bear on the Fanshawe I was writing about in the first place. I just loved the way it sounded, that plain Fanshawe, with its forceful, unclut-tered, Waspy, masculine brio—like something you'd call a classmate in a good preparatory school. Begin a story with a single name like that and, why, the thing practically writes itself! Or so I believed at the time.

And what (by the way) of Fanshawe's mother, Fanshawe—that plucky woman who died of plaid? People of my acquaintance in the medical profession assure me that, un-likely as it sounds, one can indeed die of a toxicity caused by both type and number of plaids, their juxtaposition on the skin, and other factors. What is quite a bit murkier is the ex-act sequence of events, because the body was found to have a broken neck, doubtless the result of the fall. Apparently, she had been shot repeatedly at close range as well. Whether the plaid reaction, of which there was abundant evidence, oc-curred before or after the neck was broken and the bullets fired cannot be determined by the available technologies. All may be as the report first stated, with plaid as the innocent cause. Fanshawe (orig. guy) wonders about this every day, as do, I'm sure, the innumerable other Fanshawes, though you will have to ask them yourself. None of them, including Fan-shawe, are still speaking to me.

Remembering Justice Stevens

During the two years I spent clerking for Justice John Paul Stevens—years I still consider the most memorable of my adult life—I came to know him not only as a brilliant legal mind but also as a human being. The majesty of the Supreme Court affects different justices differently; weighted by their power and responsibility, some become remote, austere, and unapproachable. That was never Justice Stevens's way. In all his dealings, he remained the amiable and unassuming person he had been while growing up in the Midwest, and he took a personal interest not only in the clerks who worked for him but also in those assigned to the other justices as well. Any of us who had questions about the law or Supreme Court protocol always knew we could go to him.

One instance of Justice Stevens's kindness and consideration stands out with special vividness in my mind. It was at the very beginning of my clerkship, when I and all the other clerks (some twenty-six in number, as I recall) received an invitation to a gala event in the White House Rose Garden celebrating the issuance of a new postage stamp in honor of John Marshall, the great chief justice and advocate of federalism. The president, Jimmy Carter, was to give a speech, along with members of Congress, the head of the U.S. Postal Service, and the chief justice (who at that time was Warren Burger). Asking around among my fellow clerks, I found that we all shared a similar confusion. What were we expected to do at this ceremony? How were we to conduct ourselves? In a condition approaching terminal stage fright, we sought out Justice Stevens and put our questions to him. He reassured us with a friendly smile that made light of our concerns while avoiding any trace of condescension. "Don't worry, fellows. Leave it to me," he said. "With the other justices, I will be standing right in front of you. Just keep your eyes on me, and do exactly what I do." This allayed our fears, and we promised to follow his instructions to the letter.

The ceremony took place on a mild afternoon in early June. The Marine Corps band was playing, the sun was smiling down, the Rose Garden roses bloomed splendidly. All nine Supreme Court justices, imposing in their long black robes, stood in a line to the right of the speaker's platform. We clerks had been placed in two lines just behind and to the right of them. All of us, needless to say, had our eyes glued to Justice Stevens, and observed his every move as the program began. Like him, we assumed an air of polite attention, our hands crossed sedately in front of us. But, for all our watchfulness, none of us saw the small bee that landed on Justice Stevens's collar and slipped down the back of his robe.

If we missed the bee's arrival, all of us soon witnessed its effect. After the invocation, President Carter mounted the podium and launched into a speech about the legacy of Chief Justice Marshall. A few minutes passed before Justice Stevens became aware of the bee under his shirt, just at the base of his neck. In an attempt to dislodge the insect, the justice raised his right shoulder, then his left. Faithful to our instructions, all twenty-six of us clerks immediately did the same. The tactic had no effect, however, so Justice Stevens repeated it, now moving alternating shoulders up and down more rapidly and jiggling his arms. None of us clerks quite understood how these gestures could be necessary for the ceremony, but, trusting implicitly in our kind mentor, we moved our shoulders and jiggled our arms just as he had done.

The more vigorous gyrations of Justice Stevens succeeded only in shaking the bee farther down inside his shirt, where it found a new foothold on the middle of his back along the spine. The sensation of the bee buzzing in this sensitive spot caused the justice to shimmy from head to toe. Looking over his shoulder as he shimmied uncontrollably across the Rose Garden lawn, he saw twenty-six clerks shimmying behind him, and in a near frantic attempt to get through to us began to wave his hands back and forth and cry, "No! No! Quit copying me!" We, assuming this was just part of the drill, waved our hands and cried, "No! No! Quit copying me!"

This seemed to frustrate him even more, and he practically shouted, "Listen! I'm really being serious! Forget what I told you earlier! Do not copy what I'm doing now!" All of us clerks had trained at Ivy League law schools, where the importance of carrying out original directions is strongly emphasized. "Listen! I'm really being serious! Forget what I told you earlier! Do not copy what I'm doing now!" we shouted in turn. Out of the corner of my eye, I noticed that in the confusion the president had broken off his speech and stepped to the back of the platform, where Secret Service agents with drawn guns now surrounded him. Meanwhile, a security helicopter had descended and was hovering threateningly.

Justice Stevens's career would last many more years, and he would eventually become one of the longest-serving Supreme Court justices in history. He would write a number of important opinions, and he changed some of his views over time—most significantly, those concerning the death penalty. At this defining moment in the Rose Garden, his finely balanced intellect did not fail him, and he came up with a plan to drive the bee out by employing a radical change in temperature—that is, by sitting on one of the many barbecue grills lined up on the lawn's adjoining banquet area. The grills were already sizzling hot and ready to cook the buffet-style barbecue feast that was scheduled to follow the ceremony.

But the flaw in this idea soon became obvious, for, as he sat, smoke began rising from his robes, until Justice Stevens suddenly burst out with "Ay, chihuahua!" At once, an echoing "Ay, chihuahua!" escaped the throats of twenty-six clerks, all of us on our own grills and all by now similarly singed. The justice then leaped from his perch and ran pell-mell in a circle through the gathering, trailing smoke and a train of equally smoky clerks, until he, and we, plunged behind-first into a moat-like trough containing melting ice and bottled beverages at the foot of a twenty-foot-high ice sculpture of the post office eagle situated near the end of the lawn. Upon our contact with the cold water, steam went up, along with a loud *sssssssssssss* that cut through the background noises of the helicopter and the excited crowd.

After my clerkship with Justice Stevens ended, I went to work for Skadden, in the mass torts division, but I soon began to drift away from the law. As the result of a long period of reflection and self-examination, I decided to change direction and go back to law school, figuring that it would be easier the second time and I wouldn't really have to study. This proved to be correct; I regraduated from Yale, then attended and graduated from the law schools of Princeton, Harvard, and Brown. As the possessor of five identical law degrees, I saw that my logical next step should be clerking for a justice of the Supreme Court. I did not apply to Justice Stevens, however, because after the incident in the Rose Garden we could never meet each other's eyes. Instead I applied to, and was accepted by, Chief Justice Hulk Hogan. Only many years later did I discover that he was not connected with the Supreme Court at all. For this reason, and for many others, I will always be grateful to have known Justice John Paul Stevens.

In My Defense

On membership applications, Boy Scouts and adult leaders must say they recognize some higher power, not necessarily religious. "Mother Nature would be acceptable," [a Boy Scout executive] said . . . The organization bans gays and atheists.

—Associated Press, 2002

As your now former scoutmaster, I hope all the members of Troop 345 and your moms and dads will put up with one last email from me. Since the Chief Seattle Council reviewed my case and handed down its decision that I was unfit to command Troop 345, I have been going over and over this whole business in my mind. Some of you are of the opinion that my emails were what got me in trouble in the first place. You may be right. But whatever I said, I said from the heart, and that's how I'm speaking to you today.

When I filled out the application to serve as your scoutmaster, I answered honestly and fully in the section about religious beliefs and affiliations, affirming that I had a deep faith in a tripartite divinity—Father, Son, and Holy Spirit. No problems there, as the Chief Seattle higher-ups assured me. Soon after, unfortunately, at about the time we were planning the light bulb drive, I happened to stumble onto some old books in my uncle's garage. While reading them, I became at first interested in, and then infected by, a pernicious false doctrine known as the Nestorian heresy.

I don't know if many of you are familiar with the incorrect teachings of Bishop Nestorius, Patriarch of Constantinople, for which he and his followers were condemned by the Council of Ephesus in 431. Don't worry if you're not, because the question of the double nature of the Son (divine and human, or divine *or* human), which Nestorius raised, is really neither here nor there. I'm just trying to convey what was in my head as we canvassed all of Bremerton pushing those light bulbs—of which we sold a ton, I'm happy to say, and raised almost $875 in a single weekend!

The danger of heresies, as I hope none of you will ever find out for yourselves, is that one leads to another. As my attraction to Nestorianism began to fade, I found myself strangely intrigued by the Petrobrusian heresy (anti-infant baptism, anti-sacraments), and from that I segued easily into the Pelagian heresy, tempting to me because of its bold rejection of the whole concept of original sin. Soon after my Pelagian period, I did a 180 and became a strict Augustinian (i.e., not a heretic at all), but that didn't last long, because then I was up to my ears in Patripassianism, a sneaky heresy that says the Father shared the Son's earthly sufferings voluntarily. For a while there, I was going through heresies one or two a week—Arianism, Dualism, Quietism, Socinianism, Anabaptism, the Bogomil heresy, Albigensianism—nothing was too undoctrinal for me. Looking back, I now regret these excesses. However, I will submit to all of you who love Troop 345 as I do that none of my spiritual wanderings or errors in those days affected my performance as your scoutmaster.

If you were very observant, you might have noticed that I did make a few minor changes to my uniform as secret reminders to myself of whatever heresy I was into at the time. For example, I moved my scoutmaster insignia patch from my right pocket to my left and sewed it on upside down to suggest a brief flirtation with Manichaeism. Similarly, I went from the standard, two-hole neckerchief slide to a hand-tooled three-hole model for obvious trinitarian reasons, and I affected gold shoulder cords, perhaps excessively, during my lapse into free-grace Arminianism. All harmless enough, I'm sure you'll agree.

Some of the scouts and dads who attended my Know Your Knots master class at the Camp Shoshone Summer Jubilee later remarked that I had seemed distracted when I gave it, and I consider this a fair criticism. In my defense, right at that moment I was wrestling with Valentinian Gnosticism, a real bear of a heresy. Part of me still felt strongly that every scout should be able to tie a bowline knot around his waist in the dark with one hand. But if basic Gnostic teachings were to prove well-founded, and all matter, and even creation itself, turned out to be essentially and irredeemably corrupt—well, part of me couldn't help wondering, What's the point?

Here matters stood in the fall of last year, when my spiritual life underwent a drastic shock. A book came into my possession—and I won't say how, wishing to implicate no one but myself—entitled *God Is Not Great*, by Christopher

Hitchens. I began reading it in awful fascination, frightened to continue but unable to look away. Page after page, I argued, I resisted; but the insidious, atheistical arguments drew me in. A few stubborn shreds of my belief still remained, when, on page 90, I came across these words:

How can it be proven in one paragraph that this book [the Bible] was written by ignorant men and not by any god? Because man is given "dominion" over all beasts, fowl and fish. But no dinosaurs or plesiosaurs or pterodactyls are specified, because the authors did not know of their existence.

This hit me like a blow on the head. Yes, why *are* there no dinosaurs in the Bible, if God wrote it? How could an all-knowing being leave out something so huge? That's worse than a slipup; it smacks of carelessness—even ignorance, as Hitchens says. And if Adam and Eve actually did have "dominion," why didn't they ride around Eden on a dinosaur? Nothing adds up here. At first, grasping at straws, I told myself the omission might be the result of a copyist's error in the Middle Ages. But that didn't comfort me for long. Too many other really big things are left out also, like manatees, for example. Or what about elephant seals, the largest meat eaters on the planet, which can grow to more than six thousand pounds?

Yet if God did not write the Bible (my own fevered thoughts continued), he certainly did take credit for it. That is, God did not go out of his way to make it clear that he had *not* written this book attributed to him. Quite simply, he appropriated work done by someone else. And, if that weren't bad enough, he never even checked these scriptures to see if his ghostwriters got the facts halfway right. He did not appear in a vision to suggest they needed to add a dinosaur or some trilobites for realism. As I noticed with newly opened eyes all that was left out of this book, I had to admit an even more upsetting possibility: not only did God not write or check the Bible; it's quite likely that he did not even read the whole thing. I began to ask myself if I could believe in a God like that—one who plagiarized, and did it so sloppily and disrespectfully. I reached the painful conclusion that I could not.

Now I was in a predicament. In just a week, Troop 345 was scheduled to begin its annual Frozen Turkey Roundup in conjunction with the outreach program at St. Barnabas. And here Troop 345's scoutmaster had become an atheist! I had no time to lose. Sitting down at the computer, I composed a long and detailed email to the district council explaining everything, through all the various heresies, the dinosaurs, manatees, etc., up to my current loss of faith. I sent it off and expected a call within the hour, so we could start looking for my replacement. Instead, a couple of days went by. Finally, the council sent me an email that I found both mystifying and beside the point. They made almost no mention of my spiritual crisis, merely stating that I could stay on if I recognized some higher power, or even Mother Nature! Were they kidding? After all the subtle and wicked heresies I had defeated, did they think I would fall into plain old nature-worshipping Druidism and grow a white beard and harvest mistletoe?

All of you know what happened next. I sent out the mass email to every member of the district council, to all my scouts and their families, and to both of the local newspapers. I then received notice from the council that my tenure as scoutmaster was terminated, effective immediately. By now you all know, too, of the vision I had that restored my faith. So glorious was this miracle for me that I don't care what it makes anyone think. The series of emails I sent immediately afterward described it in full. I am aware that heresies often come escorted by false prophets, and I have no wish to be a prophet, false or otherwise; I am merely trying to impart that which I personally saw. An angel hovering over my backyard on a snow-white pterodactyl would arouse anybody's skepticism, even (at first) my own. All I can say is, this angel really knew his dinosaurs! In fact, he could have been a docent at the Dinosaur Museum of the Rockies, with the abundance of information he possessed. I also believe, with every fiber of my being, that the lost Dinosaur Scrolls he told me about do exist, somewhere in the Sinai Desert, and will be discovered someday.

In the Boy Scout Oath, each of us promises "to do my duty to God and my country." And wasn't that what I was doing as I struggled through thickets of heresy into the light, and as I worked on my ongoing project to reinsert dinosaurs into the Holy Book, based on some of the things the angel told me, along with ideas I came up with on my own? I want to be your scoutmaster again, more than I can say. Even assistant scoutmaster would be acceptable, if I could add a role as troop chaplain, with opportunity for advancement possibly all the way to the top at the Boy Scouts' national headquarters. If all the scouts and parents from Troop 345 accompany me to the next session of the Chief Seattle Council, and everybody raises a demonstration for my reinstatement, I am sure the council will agree. In the name of God, scouting, and the apatosaurus, I ask for your support.

A Bow to Our Benefactors

The Queens County–Abilify Library Museum and Center for the Performing Arts has been unusually blessed with financial angels who shelter us under their collective wing, and we wish to take a moment to recognize them here. Like most cultural institutions of its kind, the QC-ALM&CPA literally would be unable to function without the kindness and generosity of our donors. To put it plainly, we owe them our lives. The sad part, however, is that although visitors to our facility see the names of these individuals gracing our walls, door lintels, exit signs, and other flat surfaces, they don't know, and rarely stop to inquire as to who these wonderful people are. For that regrettable ignorance the following is a small attempt at a remedy.

Why not start with me, the QC-ALM&CPA's executive director, Sandor A. Stattsman-not? Though not an actual wealthy donor myself, I proudly bear the name of one. Every year, auctioning off the privilege of renaming me provides our institution with a welcome revenue stream. The addition of a simple "not" at the end of my new moniker solves the minor problem of staff and others confusing me with this year's outstanding top bidder, Mr. Sandor A. Stattsman. Mr. Stattsman has expressed great satisfaction with customizing his giving in this way, and my wife, Mrs. Sandor A. Stattsman-not, gets a kind of kick out of it, too. It has been more difficult for the children. But until the end of my tenure we as a family are the Sandor A. Stattsman-nots, and so we shall remain!

My namesake, the distinguished Mr. Sandor A. Stattsman himself, is a delightful human being. His partner, the equally delightful Carla (Kit) Stattsman, once inspired me to remark that although Sandor has the Kit, we're hoping someday to get the caboodle! However, neither of them is very old. Mr. Stattsman's former firm does financial-consulting work for financial-sector financing. He is retired now and whittles pieces from soap.

Those of you who entered our physical plant through the street entrance may have parked in the AAA Overflow Vehicle Area. This name has nothing to do with the automobile club—a common mistake. Underwriting for the repaving of this region was provided anonymously, with the condition that the donor's middle initial be used three times on the sign. As you step from your car, please take a moment to examine the yellow line separating the parking space you have chosen from the one beside it. Like all the other parking space lines, yours bears a small plaque with the name of Sandor A. Stattsman. In this instance, he did not actually pay anything; he just wanted his name there. He is the same Sandor A. Stattsman as was referred to above.

Mr. Stattsman did, however, donate the curb, henceforth known as the Sandor A. Stattsman Curb. If you get down on your hands and knees on our lawn and take out your magnifying glass or jeweler's loupe, you'll notice that every blade of grass has been inscribed with the name of each individual grass seed's donor, Sandor A. Stattsman. The engraving was done using complicated techniques involving gene splicing and recombinant DNA. Mr. Stattsman would also want me to mention that he can clean-and-jerk 250 pounds and is *un homme formidable* (fr.).

Interestingly, several parts of our facility are not directly named for Sandor A. Stattsman. The Francis and Adele Kuhn Miller Three-Foot Ledge, for example, commemorates a lengthy lunch with Francis and Adele Kuhn Miller, from whom a donation was extracted much as one might remove a decaying molar with a pair of long-handled pliers. If you are eager to learn about the difficulty of trying to get patio chairs re-caned in a fourth home on a Caribbean island, the Millers are the folks for you. Mr. and Mrs. F. V. Spaethe, local burglars and day traders, gave the section of ledge just beyond the Millers'. The Spaethes' brass nameplate came out somewhat smaller, owing to a sizing error, and it was STOP PAYMENT, MR. BANKER! Clemont Hamps, of the Southampton Hampses, provided the funds for the left-hand banister on our main staircase. This furnishing was cast from platinum-bronze alloy in a precise replica of Mr. Hamps's distinctive signature. The banister on the right, currently consisting of taped-together mailing tubes, still awaits a sponsor. Do I see any takers out there?

As I look from the window of my office on the third floor of the under-construction Stattsman Wing, I feel great pride in what we have accomplished. I remember the many checks that cleared, and those that did not. A hundred million dollars, for example, is an absolutely lovely amount of money, if anybody wants to give it to me. It consists of a one with two zeros, a comma, and six other zeros, and then on the line below it you write, "ONE HUNDRED MILLION AND NO HUNDREDTHS of" next to the word "dollars," already printed on the check. I would be happy to do the clerical work of filling that in myself, if you prefer.

I know that every one of our donors believes in the mission of our institution just as I do, and for that I am profoundly grateful. At no time during my directorship have I or any of my staff felt the least pressure from any donor, funder, grant-awarding organization, or high-net-worth individual to alter or interfere with QC-ALM&CPA policy in any way. Mr. Sandor A. Stattsman in particular gives me a completely free hand as long as I ask ahead of time, and I think our health and vitality reflect that. Last year, when Mr. Stattsman stated publicly that raising the federal income tax on capital gains from 15 percent to 15.25 was like the Soviet invasion of Yugoslavia, the excitement it caused in the media made barely a ripple here.

Our subsequent decision, as a cultural institution, to place on our building's roof a hundred-foot red and orange neon sign saying CAP. GAINS TX. INCREASE = SOV. INVASION Y'SLAVIA has no connection to or bearing upon Mr. Stattsman, and we deny any such implication. We stand by our sign proudly as a creative choice that came from inside ourselves. Mr. Stattsman's later gift to me of a toaster oven was just a coincidence because I cleaned his pool. So three hearty hurrahs for Mr. Stattsman and our other marvelous donors, or however many hurrahs they want! Please let me know if there's anything else I can do.

Messages from Dr. Abravenel

"Monday, October 17, 12:47 p.m."

"Hello, Mr. Singer, this is your physician, Dr. Morris Abravenel, calling with your test results, and I'm just as glad, quite frankly, not to find you in. This way, I can be brief. I am out of the office myself at the moment, on the back nine at Indian Balls Golf Club here in Palm Desert, fourteenth hole, which is a beautiful little par-3, a hundred and forty-two yards, and I'll be hitting a five iron, as my caddy, Arturo, recommends. There are some slow players ahead of us, so I've got a minute here—Play through! Play through!—and on top of that we've got some fast players behind us! What a headache. So I'm just going to let them play through while I turn to the important subject of what your test results are telling me. I'll be very straight with you, Mr. Singer. These are some disturbing numbers you have here, and your X-rays, which Arturo is now holding up to the gorgeous Palm Desert sun so I can examine them more closely, seem to indicate—"

Beep. "Memory bank full."

"Tuesday, October 18, 8:50 a.m."

"Mr. Singer, it's Dr. Abravenel again, returning your calls. Your tape ran out on me yesterday. So, in regard to your test numbers and X-rays, as I was saying, I do see some areas for serious concern. The main problem is that I'm bringing the club back too quickly. I need to slow the backswing down, because when I come forward my hips are not ahead of the club face, and— Excuse me, Mr. Singer, the starter is asking me something. It's tournament week here, and . . . Mr. Singer, this is a very inconvenient time for me to have called you. Would you mind having a seat in your apartment? I'll be with you shortly. Maybe there's a magazine you can read. Thank you."

"Tuesday, October 18, 4:03 p.m."

"Mr. Singer, Dr. Morris Abravenel. Just a quick message about your test results, so as not to keep you waiting. I want you to know that there's no need to worry about them, after all. I've lost them. They disappeared somewhere, and your X-rays, too. It's been windy as hell here at Indian Balls all day, stuff blowing everywhere, and, would you believe it, at one point this afternoon they even had to suspend play! Normally it's so beautiful here. But I did want to put your mind at rest about that."

"Tuesday, October 18, 10:15 p.m."

"False alarm, Mr. Singer—your test results weren't lost, as it turns out. I had put them in another player's golf cart, and this evening he kindly returned them to the very comfortable condo belonging to my ex-wife's brother where I am staying here at Indian Balls. So, going over the results and the X-rays—and I kind of hate to tell you this straight out in a message on an answering machine, but—well, Mr. Singer, your condition appears to be very, very serious, possibly terminal. So that's the bad news.

The good news is, you would not believe the day I just had. I am playing the best golf of my life. Maybe it was the way the grass blades on the greens were bent or something that was slowing my putt down, but I was drilling those eight-footers, Mr. Singer, just *draining* them! I could do no wrong. So take heart—all is not gloom and doom. We'll talk later in the week."

"Friday, October 21, 12:22 p.m."

"Hello, Mr. Singer, this is Dr. Morris Abravenel, calling in reply to your last several telephone messages, and all I can say, Mr. Singer, is: Wow! What lung power! I don't usually give a diagnosis over the phone, but you certainly *sound* healthy, no matter how deathly ill your test results might indicate that you are. And, about your comment that you plan to sue me, please be advised that I have had myself registered as a Liberian national with diplomatic immunity, so, if you do go to court, I believe you will find that you have no standing. However, I sense something in your tone that makes me a bit apprehensive, so to avoid miscommunication I am sending you my bill right away for services rendered so far. Justin, the young man in the pro shop, is letting me use his fax machine, so it should be coming through any minute now at your end."

FAX TRANSMISSION FROM:

Dr. Morris Abravenel, MD, PC, LLD, Lwn. Dr.
Starter's Booth
Back Nine
Indian Balls Golf Course

Palm Desert Enclave (gated)

Palm Desert, CA 92210

————————

Patient	Mr. Singer
Insurer	Visa or MasterCard
Billing Cycle	24–7–365

Procedure	*Fee*
Lumbar manipulation (by phone)	$2,200.00
Colonoscopy (subcontracted)	5,035.00
Telephone consultation (not home)	175.00
Telephone consultation (home)	500.00
Perform implant (by remote)	7,500.00
Redo implant (on-site)	22,500.00
Airfare	1,380.00
Lodging	765.48
Taxis	235.00
Meals	378.43
Equipment rental	350.00
Deposition (@$600/hr.)	1,200.00
Breakage and Misc.	8,000.00
New balance	$50,218.91

Detach for your records

OWED INSTANTLY TO DR. MORRIS ABRAVENEL: $50,218.91

Please!!

END OF FAX TRANSMISSION

———

"Monday, October 24, 3:18 p.m."

"Well, hello again, Mr. Singer, and, boy, is my face red! Owing to a reshuffling of our filing system, the records I thought were yours actually belonged to a Mr. Edmund Singer, a patient who is, uh . . . well, who happens to be deceased. This is what comes of not leaving your first name when you call. So what I was assuming were your test results was actually this patient's autopsy report, and that accounts for my rather grim prognosis. Well, no harm, no foul, Mr. Singer. I have no idea of your current state of health, but at least you can't be as bad off as this poor fellow! And about my bill: since it's already in the system, the best thing for you to do is just pay it, and then talk to my secretary and the insurance companies and, possibly, obtain a reimbursement later. That will avoid any problem with the collection agencies.

"Not that this constitutes in any way an admission of error on my part, but, to show that there are no hard feelings, how would you like to come out here on your own nickel and play a round as my guest at Indian Balls? Let me know if that works for you. Till then, take care, and goodbye from your physician, Dr. Morris Abravenel."

99% Chance

Joel Klein declared only a handful of snow days in his 8½-year reign as New York City schools chancellor . . . One of them was to make good on a promise he made to Caroline Kennedy Schlossberg's son, Jack . . . Klein said the boy [asked] him, "Will you declare a snow day on my birthday?"

—*New York Daily News*

New York City Public Schools

CALENDAR OF CLASSES AND EVENTS FOR THE COMING SCHOOL YEAR:

(Parents and caregivers, please note that school starts one week early this year, to allow for highly likely weather-related closures.)

August 25—Thursday. All staff report. Preparation of classrooms, professional development. Distribution of "Severe Weather Readiness" packets.

September 1—Thursday. School opens for all students not at Brearley, Buckley, Chapin, Collegiate, Dalton, Fieldston, Hewitt, Packer, Nightingale, Spence, Trinity, etc. (For full list, see appendix.)

September 5—Monday. Labor Day. Schools closed. Last day of Hampton Jitney summer schedule.

September 8—Thursday. School opens for all students at Brearley, Buckley, Chapin, Collegiate, Dalton, Fieldston, Hewitt, Packer, Nightingale, Spence, Trinity, etc., if quite convenient.

September 29, 30—Thursday, Friday. Rosh Hashanah. Schools closed, unless opened by phone call.

October 10—Monday. Columbus Day. Schools probably closed, depending on phone call from important friend.

October 25—Tuesday. Expect possible closure due to heavy fall leaf accumulation (and paper due 10/26, AP U.S. History, Chapin).

November 9—Wednesday. Public schools may be closed, owing to possibility of thick fog or maybe sleet. (Buckley-Spence-Collegiate-Dalton lacrosse-tourney playoffs.)

November 11—Friday. Veterans Day. Schools closed, assuming that's okay with whoever's running the schools in New York City.

November 24, 25—Thursday, Friday. Thanksgiving. Schools almost certainly closed.

November 28—Monday. Schools possibly closed because of solar flare advisory. (Jet-lag day, École Internationale, Lycée Français.)

December 15—Friday. Preemptive school closure because of high statistical slush probability. (Broker-student in-office conference hours—Fieldston, Collegiate, Chapin, Packer.)

December 18–January 2—Schools closed for holiday recess, but we can be flexible, if you want to get into one and have a silent auction or a Christmas luau or something.

January 16—Monday. Dr. Martin Luther King Jr. Day. Schools definitely closed.

January 27—Friday. Wow, what a snowstorm might happen at this time of year! Better not to have school. (Joint Chapin-Marymount-Spence musicale on the slopes in Stowe, Vermont: "A Snow Day Would Be Awfully Rich Right Now!")

February 20–24—Monday through Friday. Midwinter recess. Schools closed, but not necessarily.

March 23—Friday. It sometimes snows this late, right? So—NO SCHOOL! (Riverdale Country varsity polo team to sectionals, Saint-Tropez.)

April 6–13—Friday through Friday. Easter, Passover. Schools closed, but available for whatever. Make offer.

April 23—Monday. Mandatory system-wide viewing (via Skype) of presentation by former schools chancellor Joel Klein: "Rupert 'n' Me: Why I'm Lovin' My News Corp Boss."

May 21—Monday. Anticipated school closure because that volcano in Iceland might erupt again. (5/22 deadline for major, major science project determining one-half of final grade, with college entrance implications, Junior AP Bio, Horace Mann.)

May 28—Monday. Memorial Day. First day of Hampton Jitney summer schedule.

June 7—Thursday. Chancellor's Conference Day for staff development relating to Regents Examinations and making important contacts (see presentation of former chancellor, above). Schools closed, but don't quote us.

June 20—Wednesday. Schools closed as a result of excessively unthreatening weather, because that's just when the worst storms hit—when you don't expect them. (Dalton golf team makeup final exam on 6/21 in Human Studies, which will probably be really hard and they will have to study a lot for.)

June 27—Wednesday. LAST DAY FOR ALL STUDENTS. 1:30 p.m. dismissal, except for students at Brearley, Buckley, Chapin, Collegiate, Dalton, Fieldston, Hewitt, Packer, Nightingale, Spence, etc., who of course are free to leave whenever they choose.

June 28, 29—Thursday, Friday. All staff report for performance review, return of unused sacks of sidewalk de-icer, *Farmers' Almanacs*, foul-weather gear. See you next fall (conditions permitting)!

Cranial Fracking

Recently, I signed a lease with a major oil company allowing it to begin "cranial fracking"—deep drilling to tap the vast reserves of natural gas found in the human head. These reserves are not distributed uniformly in all individuals. In my case, however, a gas-rich formation known as the Jersey Deposit runs from behind my eyebrows to beneath my bald spot and then angles downward to the point of my chin. According to the prospecting crews, this cranial structure holds enough CH_4 (methane) to power all of New England for twenty to fifty years. When this bonanza was discovered, oil company representatives came to me hoping to lock in permanent and exclusive extraction rights for a fee that was truly eye-popping (although that may also have been a result of the seismic "thumper trucks" they used).

As the details were explained, I wished I had paid more attention during the brief cranial section of my earth sciences class in high school. Apparently, back in the Silurian period, some 438 million years ago, my head was completely covered by a shallow inland sea. In time, the sea receded and swampy Carboniferous growth sprang up. In the resultant ooze, distinct parietal ridges appeared, trapping some of the carbon. Ages passed, I was officially born, there was that difficult year of kindergarten, and very slowly, under extreme pressure, valuable gas was formed. I have suspected its existence since about the fourth grade. I was hammering a nail into my nostril, just to see what would happen, as kids will do, when suddenly there was a tremendous explosion that sent nail and hammer flying and injured a neighbor in his yard across the street. After that, I knew I was different, although I wasn't sure I wanted to be. But now, like thousands of similar people, I count myself somewhat lucky to possess this resource.

Getting at it has always been the hard part. With some guys (and most of those whose heads contain the Jersey Deposit formation are men, curiously), a gas seep rises clear to the surface of the head. Then all that the extraction workers have to do is part the hair (where there is hair) and screw a well cap and valve directly into the skull. With me and others like me, however—not so easy. First, entry sites must be established just at the front of each ear, where the overburden is shallow and the head is narrowest. Then multidirectional diamond-tipped drills bore through the obstructing bone until they reach the remote inner levels, where the richest concentrations of gas lie hidden. Often, this is a hit-or-miss process. A moment's inattention on the part of the drilling technician, who is sitting at a console in his apartment and also checking his email, can cause mistakes. The bit may emerge unexpectedly, scattering skull fragments, and plunge onward through one's hat or glasses, as has happened on more than one occasion to me, I am sorry to say.

Quite honestly, the whole process hurts like bloody hell. After the drill has reached the gas deposits, contained in thousands of tiny pockets no more than a few molecules across, the surrounding bone must be microscopically shattered to free them. This is done by backing out the drill, taping on a small firecracker, lighting it, shoving it back in the well bore, and shouting, "Fire in the hole!" After a muffled sound, smoke comes out, sometimes accompanied by bits of teeth and brain lining, depending on how accurately the charge has been shaped. I don't have to tell you that this is the moment when I must keep our country's energy future in mind in order to withstand the horrible agony. Also, unavoidably, some of the gas escapes before the well can be capped and hooked into the distribution network. Cranial gas is itself a very potent agent of climate change, and my own, as it turns out, is considerably worse than most.

A stream of surfactant at very high PSI is then shot back into the well bore to flush it, and the fluid is sealed up permanently in skull chambers, sometimes causing temporary dizziness and nausea. This fluid-containment system ensures that nothing will ever come out, although in the unlikely (but not uncommon) event that it does migrate into your mouth, it tastes like pineapple. Reports have said that a flammable facial exudate possibly also results from this process, though no connection has been found.

Until the past few years, none of the technologies I've described were available. If you had a head full of top-grade crude, you simply went to the squasher and, one-two, you were done. Back then, nobody bothered about utilizing other cranial hydrocarbons, because there was no need. Today, the equipment is so sophisticated that it can find a single molecule of gas in a head of almost solid bone, like Senator Inhofe's. However, I am not blind to the controversies— that is, when the pumping mechanism is working properly and I'm not blind for other reasons. I know that people have made negative comments, which are right, but they are not the ones who know about this personally and are getting paid. Yes, everything now tastes like pineapple to me, and there's the pain, and I have these Christmas-tree valve arrays that make it impossible to fly on airplanes, and my pores combust spontaneously if I don't keep the moistened towels on, but I recommend the procedure without reservation.

The only thing I would say is, if you are thinking of putting your signature on a cranial-gas lease agreement, it's best to wait until the kids are grown and out of the house. If you have a spouse or a domestic partner, separate, and obtain a divorce if necessary. You will want to spend all your time in a corrugated-metal building with an oil-soaked earthen floor. Find a good oil-patch lawyer and have him begin proceedings against you as a preventive measure. Direct wire transfer of lease monies to the Caymans is the only way to go. And here's a secret: guy wires. Attached from your head to a building's rafters, they provide neck support that feels wonderful. You will thank me down the road.

All Mine

Tax the rich! That's always the answer, isn't it? You get yourself in over your head with your foolish economics and right away you run to the rich to make everything all right. Now, we know that taxing the rich won't make a dent in the deficit. In fact, tax the rich and you'll actually have *less* money than before, because the rich will simply move their money, and they'll stop creating catering and florist jobs, and all the jeweled-egg factories will close, and millions if not billions will be thrown out of work—I mean literally, physically thrown. Job creation, and Creation itself, will stop. This is as plain as kindergarten, but do people remember the consequences when the rich are taxed? Sadly, they do not.

There's no mystery about how it works. Human beings have always known, but they conveniently choose to forget. In the Bible, we remember Jonah. He was a man who taxed the rich, and—*bam!*—eaten by a whale. A parable, maybe, but one with an important truth. The Trojan Horse was an idea that the Trojans fell for because they thought, wrongly, as it turned out, that having a Trojan Horse would somehow help them tax the rich. Not the smartest move, after all! Like Warren Buffett, Julius Caesar believed that it would be a swell policy to tax people like himself—i.e., the rich—and got some knives in his inner organs from his rich friends who thought, Hey, you want to pay taxes so bad, write a check yourself, Caesar! Charlemagne taxed the daylights out of the rich but got away with it—the exception that proves Milton Friedman—but not King Charles XII of Sweden! Ask him what taxing the rich did for him at the Battle of Poltava. That is, if you can find his scattered bones and the badly shredded financial records of his reign.

In America, we know better than to tax the rich. Or do we? Ask wised-up rich-taxers like Hale Boggs and Amelia Earhart. Abraham Lincoln, on the night he went to Ford's Theatre, made some marks on paper which, though they said something else, may actually have been a plan to "pay for the war" by taxing the rich. I put that phrase in quotes because not once in human history has taxing the rich ever paid for a war. In fact, it has in every instance made wars impossible to pay for. Lincoln's subsequent death at the hands of an assassin had an ironic twist, in that John Wilkes Booth would have gotten clean away had he not made the ill-advised decision to send in an absentee ballt in Harf0rd C0unty in which he v0ted in fav0r 0f a b0nd issue that w0uld tax the rich. Traced t0 the barn where he was hiding, B00th himself was heavily taxed and then burned and sh0t and p0ssibly diss0lved in p0ts 0f s0dium hydr0xide.

The f0urth v0wel, the 0ne y0u need t0 spell "0h!," has br0ken 0n this h0rrible typewriter I have been pr0vided with t0 write what y0u, my "capt0rs" (we will see ab0ut that!), call my "final financial statement" (ha!), s0 I am n0w f0rced t0 use the numeral 0. N0thing daunted, I g0 0n. Let us never f0rget Jim Th0rpe, wh0 w0n l0ts 0f 0lympic medals, subsequently taken away by a c0nfiscat0ry tax 0n g0ld.

N0 greater injustice has ever been cOmmitted 0n American 0il. 0h, hell, n0w the letter in the alphabet between "r" and "t" ha$ br0ken. I meant t0 $ay, "0n American $0il."

Tax the rich? It will $imply never fly, becau$e 0f 0ur di$tinctly American ene 0f fairne$$. H0w fair i$ it 0f y0u t0 gang up, when there are nine hundred and ninety-nine 0f y0u f0r every 0ne 0f me? H0w w0uld y0u like it if nine hundred and ninety-nine rich pe0ple ganged up 0n each 0f y0u? I am n0t afraid t0 call what y0u have d0ne—invading my wealthy Zip C0de, burning d0wn all h0ue with fl00r $pace 0f m0re than twenty th0u$and $quare feet, and making me y0ur "captive"—by it$ rightful name, which i$ cla$$ warfare. And yet, f0r all y0ur $trength in number$ and y0ur mi$guided p0licie$, y0u $till have n0thing t0 write 0n but thi$ piece-0f-junk typewriter. Haven't y0u pe0ple ever heard 0f c0mputer$? 0bvi0u$ly, y0ur 0rganizati0n i$ a bl0ated, t0p-heavy bureaucracy in which market f0rce$ are n0t all0wed t0 w0rk pr0perly. G0d help u$ if y0u ever get near the c0ntr0l$ 0f 0ur Dem0cracy!

I am ju$t praying that the "e" d0e$n't break 0n thi$ crummy thing. Tax the rich and $00n we'll all be typing 0n n0n-c0mpetitive techn0l0gy like thi$, 0r writing with feather$. G0 ahead and try t0 tax me—take y0ur be$t $h0t! I'll m0ve my m0ney t0 the Cayman I$land$ $0 fa$t it will make y0ur head $pin! "My Cayman$, 'ti$ 0f thee, $weet land 0f taxe$ free, here c0me my fund$! Land where my taxe$ died, land that'$ ten pace$ wide, dear Cayman I$land$, h0w I tried N0t t0 pay 0ne dime!" Ye$, it'$ a beautiful c0untry, the Cayman I$land$, 0w I l0ve it—0fi, n0, tfie letter after "g" in tfie alpfiabet fia$ n0w br0ken al$0! N0w t0 make tfiat particular letter I mu$t type a letter up$ide d0wn, becau$e it l00k$ kind 0f $imilar t0 tfie letter tfiat br0ke. Wfiat a nigfitmar!

0fi, fiΣll! TfiΣ lΣttΣr I wa$ afraid w0uld brΣak fia$ br0kΣn! N0w I mu$t rΣplacΣ tfiat lΣttΣr witfi an up$idΣ-d0wn 3. Taking tfiΣ papΣr 0ut 0f tfiΣ typΣwritΣr and turning it up-$idΣ d0wn ΣvΣry timΣ I want t0 typΣ an "fi" 0r an "Σ" i$ an incrΣdiblΣ wa$tΣ 0f timΣ, but I $upp0$Σ it'$ $tandard 0pΣrating pr0cΣdurΣ f0r tfiΣ likΣ$ 0f y0u! N0w tfiΣ tab kΣy ju$t camΣ 0ff! PiΣcΣ$ arΣ flying 0ff tfii$ typΣwritΣr likΣ $firapnΣl! I d0n't carΣ! TfiΣ U.$. g0vΣrnmΣnt will nΣvΣr gΣt my m0nΣy n0 mattΣr fi0w fiard tfiΣy try! I'll $Σnd it all t0 $witzΣrland! I'll $Σnd it t0 $pacΣ in a r0ckΣt $fiip! I'll pilΣ all my m0nΣy in my yard and makΣ a big b0nfirΣ bΣf0rΣ I'll lΣt y0u l0u$y-typΣwritΣr-0wning m00cfiΣr$ gΣt y0ur grubby fiand$ 0n it! LivΣ it up and laugfi n0w, bΣ-cau$Σ vΣry $00n tfiΣ markΣt it$Σlf will pΣnalizΣ y0u! Y0u may d0 witfi mΣ wfiat y0u will, but y0u'll nΣvΣr takΣ my m0nΣy alivΣ!

Disclos'd

Scientists say some bones that were dug up in a parking lot in Leicester are those of King Richard III, the much maligned fifteenth-century monarch. The research was driven by those who believe that the king was the victim of a posthumous smear campaign.

—National Public Radio

Act V, Scene 6

Alarums. Enter King Richard.

KING RICHARD
And so at last I find an empty space
Wherein to leave my much fatiguèd horse.

Enter Richmond.

RICHMOND
Great God of Heav'n, thou foul and ill-made dog!
Canst thou not see this empty space is mine?

KING RICHARD
And how, my lord, doth this convenient space
Befit thy horse than mine more suitably?

Didst thou not see how long I sat a-saddle
Until this space's horse was gone away?

RICHMOND

Vile, lying fiend! Well dost thou know
The markings on thy horse's nearer flank
Allow for no such kind of occupancy,
Nor in this part of downtown Leicester green
Nor elsewhere here within but certain hours
Which are not now! Therefore remove thy nag
And yield my noble animal the way.

KING RICHARD

Look you, my lord, to thine own horse's markings.
The date upon its flank is long expired,
And a new surety must be obtained.
Therefore my claim and thine weigh equally.
But mine, because my wait was the longer,
Must needs outweigh the shorter wait of thine.

RICHMOND

Such low and punning words from adder's tongue
Help not thy cause, nor serve to mollify.
Remove thy beast, that mine may have this space,
Or by my sword and halberd thou shalt die!

KING RICHARD

My gentle lord, can we not get along?
'Twill take me but five minutes in yon market;
On my return, I'll give this space to thee.

RICHMOND

I truckle not with space-usurping villains!
I'll leave this life ere leave this space to thee.

Unsheath, thou loathsome, starveling, swinish elf,
Thy sword or mine shall now the case decree.

They fight.

KING RICHARD
A horse! A horse! My kingdom for a place to park my horse!

Richard is slain. Enter Lord Stanley, Earl of Derby.

DERBY
What's here, my gory Richmond? Whose pale corpse
Dost thou, so fiercely panting, now bestride?
Methinks I ken the visage of the king,
All bloodied o'er, and with his skull smashed in.

RICHMOND
The king? Art thou jesting with me, Derby?
That this man was the king I never dreamt.
Most unlike his depictions did he seem.
I am in deep and gloomy hazard, Derby,
Should this unwitting slaughter come to light.

DERBY
He was a good and kind and gallant king,
But why now tarry for the life that's spilled?
Here's a shovel, Richmond. And one for me.
Let's put him in the ground before he stiff'ns.

They bury Richard. Drums sound from afar.

RICHMOND
They come. Friend Derby, we must haste away
Lest we be apprehended and disclos'd.

The space in which he wished to rest his horse
May be his bed for yea five hundred years.
Or longer, e'en. Richard, *requiescat.*
Thy portrait to thy face was ill-adjusted;
I had not slain thee had they been more like.
Henceforth to double-proof my safety
I'll spread unrighteous slanders of thy reign.
The sapling princes vanished from the Tower
Became apprentice furriers in France,
As we now know. I'll say thou murdered them.
Small, erring details—who has time to check?
I'll heap them up to tow'rs of calumny,
Then haply pen a history untrue,
Disfiguring thy good and holy name
And leave it lying about in some near place
To trap base plagiarizers yet unborn.
Such toilsome efforts are of me required,
Because of the woeful lack of parking
In Leicestershire.

Exeunt.

Recherche

Police say a woman told a 69-year-old Florida man she was a vampire before biting off chunks of his face and part of his lip. [The man] told St. Petersburg police Thursday he was sleeping in his motorized wheelchair on the porch of a vacant Hooters when the attack happened.

—Associated Press

For a long time I used to go to bed early on the porch of a vacant Hooters. Often my eyes would close so quickly, after I turned out my little reading light, that I did not have even a moment to wonder at the strangeness of my surroundings; for in those days the demand of mine that I be put to bed with a good-night kiss from Mamma, and only on the porch of a vacant Hooters, still seemed as much a novelty to me, when I reflected upon it, as it was a puzzlement and even an annoyance to my family. Pulled back from slumber by who knows what passing train whistle or muffler noise along the thoroughfare on which this Hooters had been unwisely situated (for the route was limited-access, and only eastbound travelers could enter the parking lot without making a tortuous left-hand turn), I found myself perplexed and temporarily awake.

Had Mamma forgotten to drive into the parking lot and come onto the porch and give me my good-night kiss? But then, like an image in a gradually emerging photograph, the recent reality of that kiss, for which I had waited so greedily, reconstituted itself in my mind, there on the porch of a vacant Hooters.

My father, who was loving and kind toward me, although stern, disapproved of my sleeping arrangement, and of my kind mother's almost helpless yielding to the demands of her insistent son. My grandmother, however, said to my father, "Let the boy spend some time in the out-of-doors, because sleeping on the porch of a vacant Hooters will make a man of him!" And so it must have done, for I continued this practice throughout my youth and adulthood, and even into old age. I should add that during my faraway adolescence this particular Hooters was not, in fact, always vacant, and, when occupied and open for business, could not help but leave a strong impression upon a young man's unconscious mind—the tight daffodil-yellow shirts that the female servers habitually wore, with the two large "O"s in the middle of the word "Hooters," prominent upon their proud fronts, and the hypnotic, owl-like eyes set so arrestingly in the middle of the "O"s, working their inevitable and mysterious way into my dreams.

So it often is with our past; for this Hooters, having made its inextinguishable mark, remained itself in memory even after in its present existence it had become no more than an abandoned shell; just as Mamma has lived on in my love, fragrant in her rustling evening dress of blue muslin, long after she could no longer drive over regularly to bestow her kiss, having vanished, in mournful company with my fa-

78

ther and grandmother, finally and irretrievably from this earth. As a rule, we are better advised to let our memories remain disembodied in their penumbral chambers, and not look for their similes in the living world; and so, in retrospect, I should certainly not have sought substitutes for Mamma and her good-night blessing among the element one is likely to find upon the porch of a Hooters when that Hooters has become vacant.

And now I also begin to ask myself how I could even have imagined that a woman who might tell police she had told me she was a vampire could replicate the delightful impression of my gentle mother's lips upon my cheek. For Mamma had many unexpected qualities, but a tendency toward vampirism (much less confessing to the police) was never, so far as I can now recall, among them. Of my grandmother, however, I am less sure; I knew her only in her later years, at an age when one's early passions have cooled. Indeed, I may wonder whether her enthusiasm for outdoor sleeping on my part did not point to a previous period of nighttime activities of her own. In any case, I may say with certainty that in my grandmother's young womanhood there were no Hooterses, with porches or without, vacant or in operation, that she might have used for vampiric purposes, had she in fact possessed them—or they her, I suppose.

All is carried away by the remorseless hours. The sleep that has come and gone for me so many nights on the porch of a vacant Hooters will finally arrive with no provision having been made for its departure, and I will enter into its dark permanence in search of my dear, misunderstanding relatives, who, for once, have gone to bed earlier than I. For the moment, however, I will order the hot buffalo wings with ranch dressing (which I will no doubt regret) from an establishment nearby, along with a sleeping draught of valerian drops in water; thus do we vainly attempt to forestall our ancient enemy, time.

The Roosevelt Outtakes

[Appropriate old-timey American tune, played molto lento.*]*

NARRATOR: For over two generations, a remarkable American family was brought up to love their country and value public service, while talking incredibly, incredibly slowly. The contributions they made remain a part of our lives today and will last into eternity. This is the endless continuation of their story.

Part 15, Episode 24: "The Bad Call"

Voice of Eleanor Roosevelt: Meryl Streep

[DIRECTOR, off-mic: "So, Meryl, let's not rush this—okay?"]

Black-and-white photo of bare trees. Slow pan upward on sepia photograph of Eleanor Roosevelt's feet in oxford shoes.

ELEANOR: . . . I TOLD Franklin—
[DIRECTOR: "Hate to stop you, Meryl, but can you take the name a little slower?"]
ELEANOR: I TOLD Fran klin—
["Maybe even a little slower than that?"]
ELEANOR: I TOLD Fran klin
["Good."]

ELEANOR: I TOLD Fran klin that Mis ter *Carroll,* the COACH of the "Sea hawks," was *wrong* to call A PASS PLAY on The, One, Yard, LINE in the *Su-per* Bowl with twen ty six *seconds* remaining In The *game! BUT* Fran klin stood BY Mis ter Carroll's de cision and *said::* that of *course* the PATRI-OTS were naturally ex *pect* ing a "running" play and would have bean "stacked up" Agaynst it! So that Mis ter *Carroll* HAD made a *sen-sible* call. But::: It still did NOT seem So, TO ME. ["That's great, Meryl, but a little brisk. Bring it down just a tick next time?"]

Part 7,498, Episode 290: "The Lioness in Winter"

["Now, remember, Meryl, watch that urge to speak more than one word per second."]

Slow pan across sepia photo of Atlantic Ocean's thermohaline current coming to a stop, causing onset of another ice age.

ELEANOR: Fran klin IN SIS TED that we *keep* the *therm*-o-stat SET At no more than fif ty seven *degrees!* I, *knew* that this tem per a ture was FAR TOO CHILLY for me!!! BUT I did not say A N Y T H I N G about it. Some*times* in a *marriage* in "eternity" we must ACCEPT the other per son's idiotic "ideas" and "economies," and simply LIVE with what we are *given,* the BEST that we can.

["Good, Meryl, but can we dial the speed down just a tiny bit more?"]

Part 10^{15}, Episode 1.74 million: "The Bad Call Gets Worse"

["All the time in the universe, Meryl, so nice and easy does it."]

Slow pan across faded black-and-white photo of sun expanding to "red giant" size, having consumed all the hydrogen at its core.

ELEANOR: Fran klin and Mis ter HOWE have bean going over Mis ter *Carroll's* "bad call" in the *Super Bowl* of Two thous and Fif teen Agayn, and Agayn, and Agayn. Mis ter HOWE said the Recent AWFUL call by Quem BB1 in the Inter-Galactic Black Hole BOWL was NOTHING com pared to COACH CARROLL's "ter rib le *blunder!*" But Fran klin Said, that Mis ter Carroll had only bean "anticipating" the PATRIOTS' "run defense." And now I *find* I Have come to *agree* with Fran klin.

["That's it, Meryl. You're right on pace now."]

Part (infinite set of all prime numbers), Episode pi: "What'd I Say?"

Grainy newsreel footage of sun burning out and becoming a cinder.

["No reason to hurry now, Meryl, because time itself seems to have stopped. Whenever you're ready—"]

ELEANOR:	Fran	klin	said	to
me	that	our	little	*dog*,	Fala,
barks	so	SLOW	ly	that	by
the	time	the	Re	pub	li
cans	hear	it	an	entirely	NEW
di	men	sion	of	time	has
"taken over"	and	the	e
lec
tion	has	once	Agayn	gone	By!!

Part (larger infinity of all integers), Episode 1:

Slow pan across blackboard with complicated physics equation proving that all energy in cosmos eventually reaches absolute zero.

["Ready whenever you are, Meryl."]
["Meryl?"]
["Hello? Am I all alone here?"]

Slow pan across photo of complete nothingness, starting from the bottom.

NARRATOR: For more than two generations, a remarkable American family was brought up to love their country and value public service, while talking so incredibly slowly that matter and energy ended and no sequel could ever be made.

Walking Normally: The Facts

CLAIM: When we are at the mall you say that you have walked so much that you need to be carried, because your legs are "all stretched out."

FACT: While hyperextension of muscles, tendons, and joints is a real and serious problem among certain demographics (manual laborers, professional athletes), it is rarely seen in anyone four and a half years old.

CLAIM: Walking backward is better than walking forward.

FACT: Traditionally, human beings have walked forward rather than backward because their eyes are on the front of them and therefore can look ahead and help them see where they are going. Walking backward, as you are doing now, increases the likelihood that you will— Okay, maybe now you understand what I am trying to tell you, because you have walked backward into that lady.

CLAIM: Holding your wrists and hands up inside the sleeves of your jacket and flapping the sleeve ends back and forth when you walk somehow improves your walking, and makes you look like an elephant.

FACT: Flapping your sleeves does nothing for your walking and makes it harder for me to grab your hand when you are about to veer into a video game store where we are not going. An elephant does not flap its trunk when it walks, and, in any case, it has only one of them.

CLAIM: Skipping is faster than running.
FACT: I hate to break this to you, but skipping is actually not faster than running. It is slower. Scientists have done tests to prove this. The problem involves the added friction of the soles of the feet in the characteristic skipping motion. I know your own skipping is "special" skipping, with that extra hop that you have added in, but otherwise it is physically the same as conventional, ordinary skipping, and subject to the same laws.

CLAIM: Pressing yourself flat against the counter by the cash register, extending your arms full length, and sliding along the counter and then along the wall and then along the door until someone opens the door from the outside and you tumble out onto the sidewalk is a good way to leave a restaurant.
FACT: Look at your mother. Look at me. Look at every other human being in the world. Do we plaster ourselves against the wall and slide along it when we leave a restaurant? Why do you think nobody else does that? I don't care if Billy Nolan does it. *Nobody in his right mind does it because it is not a good way to leave a restaurant.* There is a right way and a wrong way to do everything, and sliding along flat surfaces in restaurants is generally not the right way to do anything.

CLAIM: Running very fast in circles around my legs while we are waiting for your mother by the baggage claim will hurry her arrival.

FACT: That is incorrect. There is no connection between your running and the plane that will make the plane land faster. Did you hear what I just said?

CLAIM: With the new pogo stick that your aunt gave you, you will jump over trees and houses.

FACT: No, you will not. What pogo sticks are actually good for is this: bouncing two inches off the ground once or maybe twice, and then falling over. That is it. Pogo sticks are a swindle. In the history of the world, no one has ever jumped over a house on a pogo stick. Or a tree. Or a car. Even a small car. Okay, yes—maybe a toy car. But that's not what we're talking about here. You are saying that you will go out on the driveway with your pogo stick and jump over the house, and I am saying that you will go out, get on the pogo stick, bounce once or twice, and end up still on the driveway, only with a skinned knee and screaming your head off. In this you will exactly resemble every other human who has ever attempted such a feat since the invention of the pogo stick. Your aunt gives you these things to torture me, like that life-size Earth First stuffed toy polar bear that now takes up half the living room.

CLAIM: If you're not supposed to walk backward, what about walking sideways?

FACT: No. And watch where you're going. You walked into my foot.

CLAIM: How about walking like this?
FACT: Just walk normally.

CLAIM: This *is* walking normally, for a primate.
FACT: Walk normally for a human.

CLAIM: Mrs. Varma said a human is a primate.
FACT: Yes, that is true, and just please walk normally, all right?

CLAIM: The stroller with your little sister in it will be easier for me to push if you help by pulling it from the front while singing, "Yo-ee-o, yoe, hup!"
FACT: No. Please. Stop that.

On Texas

Civics 1.0: Why We Have Texas

Did you ever stop to think about all the advantages we receive as a result of Texas? Without Texas, our government would not be able to function. To give just one example, Texas made it possible for us to have a full complement of presidents during the past fifty years. If not for Texas, we would have had to forgo the terms of Lyndon B. Johnson and George W. Bush. It was our Texas that made the existence of those presidents possible.

Or consider the space program, one of our country's proudest accomplishments. It achieved such outstanding success mainly because we, as a country, committed a sizable amount of Texas to it. Another important benefit that Texas provides is national defense. Thanks to a robust and sensible allocation of Texas, we have a military that is the envy of the entire world. It has grown to its present size and strength because of clear-sighted citizens who understood that to build a first-rate military you must have Texas. Our lives are enriched, and we live in a better and more civilized society, because of Texas.

1.1: The Cultural Rainbow Includes
Dissenting Views of Texas

Despite the obvious benefits, many Americans do not like Texas. Some even say they despise Texas, and make no secret of their feelings. They show their concern by calling for reform, while drawing attention to the fact that our Texas is very big already. Some cite studies showing that Texas in our country is already the second biggest, a finding borne out by investigation. Interestingly, they note that almost every country in the world makes do without *any* Texas. Did you know that?

1.2: A Historical Perspective

More than 170 years ago, the corrupt, undemocratic government of Mexico, unlike us, had enormous Texas. In the years that followed, the situation became reversed, and now our Texas is as big as Mexico's used to be.

1.3: Sidebar

A national pollster writes, "My firm recently selected a random sampling of passersby in Times Square and asked them how they felt about Texas. Most respondents expressed a somewhat grudging acceptance. 'Nothing you can do about Texas! Let's move on to a happier topic!' was one individual's comment, which can stand for many. Strangely, however, a few vocal outliers said they loved Texas and became irate when we could not conceal our surprise. They offered loud policy opinions, such as 'Don't mess with Texas!' or even cried, 'God bless Texas!' Such strongly held, irrational feelings would suggest little room for compromise. One interview subject went so far as to claim that he was *from* Texas—a logical impossibility, if he was not speaking metaphorically—but he was also wearing an outsize hat and sharply pointed boots, and appeared to be deliberately eccentric or perhaps insane."

1.4: A Healthy Democracy Works Toward Consensus

With careful planning, more moderate voices say, we can find an acceptable middle ground. America can enjoy a vital, fully functioning government, with all the benefits provided by Texas, while reducing Texas at the same time. Leading economists have shown that by shrinking Texas we can actually create more income for Texas in the long run. Although the notion goes against our intuition and even our common sense, we are told that smaller Texas will lead to more freedom for the average person, and thus to greater private outlays, resulting, finally, in enhanced infusions into the coffers for Texas (mostly in the form of the usual energy expenditures). The prospect is an exciting one.

1.5: Sidebar

"Now, the craziest thing we could ever do is *increase* Texas!" an influential politician says. "But, believe it or not, that's what some of the real lunatics out there want to do. For myself, and for my country, I have signed a sacred pledge that, if I ever vote to make our Texas even one tiny bit bigger than the Texas of today, I hope—I *demand*—

that my aroused and angry constituents throw me out. The thought of Texas growing and growing and ultimately consuming all of our gross national product is a cold fear that keeps me up at night. I believe Texas is the main issue confronting our country. If we don't deal with the threat of rising Texas, our children and grandchildren will find themselves in a land that is free only in name."

1.6: Conclusion and Topics for Further Study

In the changing America of today, we must allow ourselves to look at fresh ideas—in this case, to imagine Texas in new and perhaps unfamiliar ways. Try to think of what it would be like to live in an America with very, very small Texas. In this revitalized place, almost all Texas will have been eliminated. Services provided by today's bloated Texas will be taken care of more efficiently by private contractors working with volunteers, robotics, or—you fill in the details! Then, with our Texas dramatically reduced, perhaps we can phase out some of the unnecessary government officials now supported by Texas.

Imagine all that we Americans could accomplish if we never had to worry about Texas! The urge to get rid of Texas entirely is tempting, to be sure. On the other hand, if we did, might we actually start to miss Texas? Remember the benefits of Texas that we talked about before. Would we be the same country if we had no Texas? There are difficult trade-offs and serious arguments on both sides. What to do about Texas is a question that each new generation must answer for itself.

Deniers

"I accept that changes in climate are causing ocean updrafts that draw killer sharks into the atmosphere and then drop them on populated areas, but I don't believe human activity is the cause."

"Out here in Oklahoma, we have the same problems that the rest of the country is experiencing, with windborne sharks crashing through billboards and attacking folks on their way to work and so on. We have yet to see a single study, however, that connects any of these shark conditions specifically to our local fossil fuel industries."

"Tree-ring studies done on petrified wood from Utah reveal six-inch-long fossilized teeth of the megalodon, the largest shark in the history of the earth, embedded in the trunks of ponderosa pine trees more than three hundred thousand years old—trees that lived a thousand miles from the nearest ocean! So tell me: Did my SUV cause that?"

How do you get through to these people? Yes, in the past sharks have rained down numerous times, flopping around on the ground and biting early humans even in their caves—for example, as portrayed in the chilling shark attack cave paintings in Lascaux, France. Periodic showers of small but vicious Mediterranean sharks destroyed the once-proud civilization of ancient Carthage. During 1816, "the year without a summer," sharks rained on the Swiss Alps at altitudes of up to four thousand meters, ruining the vacation of Percy Bysshe Shelley and his young soon-to-be wife, Mary, and inspiring her to write her classic novel *Frankenstein vs. Jaws*. But those shark incursions into the atmosphere and onto dry land were cyclical patterns, simply a part of nature. What we are seeing today is of a whole different order of magnitude. Since the dawn of the Industrial Revolution, more sharks have been sucked up out of the ocean into waterspouts and similar weather phenomena than occurred in the previous three million years.

"We believe that God gave man dominion over the earth and all that is in it, with the exception of sharks, who have their own dominion, of course."

"If there is a problem caused by our modern technology— and I'm not necessarily saying there is—then technology will find the solution. Such as what? Such as giant shotguns, firing up at the sky constantly."

What more evidence do these people want? Ninety-seven percent of all reputable climate scientists have shot automatic rifles and shotguns at sharks plunging through the air and along the sidewalks outside their homes, classrooms, or laboratories. These men and women are trained to value empirical data, not opinions or hysteria. Almost unanimously, they have concluded that the burning of coal, oil, and natural gas at unprecedented rates is responsible, and they warn that— LOOK OUT! [*Blam blam blam blam!*]

"Our family has had sharks come through our sink drain and onto our kitchen floor, nose first, with their bloody teeth snapping, on four separate occasions. But, before we act, we need better information as to why this is."

"The shark alarmists have falsified climate-shark figures in the past."

"If there is a moderate uptick in the likelihood of a shark falling on you in North Dakota—and I am not yet convinced that there will be—remember that it will also be good for the soybeans."

When will they understand? And where do we go from here? Is there anything here we can build on? Gradually, over the next hundred years, Americans may adjust to sharks attacking them in their daily lives. On the other hand, they may decide that the situation is only marginally acceptable, and this will provide a basis for some kind of legislation. You can't change people's minds all at once. Education is the key. If there were substantially less of it, that would free up resources to make more cartridges of double-ought buckshot for when sharks are swimming up the staircase to the second floor—as they will be doing by 2025, if present trends continue. At best, that is only a temporary solution.

"We have actually had fewer sharks fall on us in the past year here in Mobile than my great-grandpa had fall on him back in 1923. Or so I've been told."

"Greta Thunberg, sharks, and Washington, D.C.—what a crew!"

"Before we go off half-cocked on the basis of a lot of

junk shark-oceanography-meteorology-science, or whatever they're calling it, let's look the facts right in the face and admit, in regard to the alleged 'shark attacks' happening all over the country every day, that it is already too late to do anything. Pass the double-ought buckshot, please."

Buds

We are not yet satisfied with the league's handling of behaviors that so clearly go against our own company culture and moral code.

—Anheuser-Busch, responding to recent scandals
in the National Football League

Wait, wait, wait! Listen, okay? Will you just—just *listen*? I love Anheuser-Busch like a brother. I've known this company all my life, or since I was eleven, when my buddies and I got some Buds and drank them. Simply a great product, a real American brand. But that's not the point. What my buddies and I consumed, way back when, just before gym class in fifth grade, along with a few shots of Old Overholt, was the Anheuser-Busch moral code. Kids today don't have that, maybe because they're not drinking enough Bud—but what do I know? I'm just one guy in a huge world. All I'm saying is, the Anheuser-Busch moral code is a part of me. That I *do* know.

You're too young to remember Spuds MacKenzie. The Budweiser dog, funny as hell, this dog danced in conga lines with beautiful "babes," as we used to call them. And he drank Bud! The dog did. Or you were supposed to *think* he did. I mean, it was just a commercial, where you can't show any person or dog actually drinking. But that's not the point. The point is this: Spuds MacKenzie was a moral dog. The moral fiber of that little animal practically jumped off the TV screen at you.

He was an inspiration to me, and to everybody, dog or human. I'm sorry, I get choked up when I think of the moral fineness of Spuds MacKenzie, and of the Anheuser-Busch company. Let me give you another example. Pine Ridge Indian Reservation, South Dakota. Just across the border, in Nebraska, a little town called Whiteclay sells more Budweiser to the Oglala Sioux than you've ever seen in your life. Budweiser beer cans all over the place, all along the road. That's not the point. The point is that with every sip of Bud, every twelve-pack, every case or car trunkful of Bud, the strictest Anheuser-Busch moral code is being imbibed.

What other company hired the theologian Paul Tillich to give it its own private moral credo? I'll answer that question for you: not a single one. Not even, technically, Anheuser-Busch—but that's not the point. Anheuser-Busch did not actually need Paul Tillich or Reinhold Niebuhr or U Thant or any of them to provide it with a solid foundation in the moral universe, because it had a pretty great morality already, which is said to be a natural by-product of the best domestic hops and beechwood aging. The original moral recipe is a secret, though.

Next round is on you. Remember? You don't? Okay, put it on my tab. "I love you, man." Now, I *know* you remember that guy. Loved his friends so much he was drinking all their Buds? A desperate alcoholic destroying all his personal relationships? He was morality, plus a beer ad.

And, I'll tell you, after I saw that ad I felt so moral that I never again committed insurance fraud except once. That was the uplifting effect Anheuser-Busch had in one man's life—my own.

But. That. Is. Not. The. Point! Point is, look at the larger picture. Anheuser-Busch is our moral beacon shining in the fog, and it is also the fog. Beacon or fog, take your pick, whatever your mood might be, this company is both. Mostly it's a beacon, though, and we should be very grateful. It's that shining brewery on a hill that Jonathan Edwards wrote about so movingly while plastered. I'm getting choked up again. I'm right, aren't I, Tommy? Of course I am.

Those great big Anheuser-Busch Clydesdales with their huge haunches and big, gorgeous, shaggy feet pulling that beer wagon through the snow every Christmas: Can you get more moral than that? Tommy, what're those feet called? Those great big, gorgeous, shaggy horse feet the Clydesdales have, with all the white fur or hair or whatever? Fetlocks? Beautiful! Tommy, you're a genius. Fetlocks! Spuds MacKenzie sometimes used to ride those horses, too. Remember that?

Shining City

Then Brother Deserve stood in the tent meeting before all the assembled brothers and sisters, and he prophesied.

"I have had a powerful vision," he said. "Here in this wilderness of the Indiana Territory, on the twentieth day of November, in the year of our Lord eighteen hundred and nine, I lay on the bare ground at the site of our future house of worship and I dreamed. A light snow fell upon me, but I noticed it not. Like Jacob of old, I put a stone beneath my head for a pillow. My badger-fur coat was my only blanket, and the stars above me were my roof. And I saw not angels in the firmament ascending and descending on a heavenly ladder, as were vouchsafed unto Jacob—no, I beheld a vision of what is to be, here, on this same prairie where we are standing, two hundred and eleven years from this very day.

"My friends, I saw the holy city of Jerusalem rising from this land! Strewn like countless jewels were the lights of her habitations, and the pleasantness of her aspects bid me enter. Hard by a wide and radiant roadway I saw a bright sign of about twenty cubits in height, and on that sign I beheld a single numeral, and a single word. The numeral, it was a seven, orange and scarlet in color; and, as for the word, it also was a number, but spelt out in glowing letters, emerald green, and those letters read ELEVEN. And the seven and the eleven were upon the sign. And the sun ascended into the firmament, above towering clouds stacked upon clouds, and shafts of brilliant sunlight shone upon the promised city. On one side of the roadway, half a furlong beyond the glowing sign, I saw many banners, as of an army, and a glorious host of conveyances—wheels next to wheels, as if of wheels there could be no end.

"And in the nearer part of this field, beside the tall windows of a crystal building, all at once a gigantic, agitated figure rose upright! Now seemingly solid, and yet somehow insubstantial, but having the general lineaments of a man, it stood suddenly with a convulsion of its spine, and flung its arms into the air, and waved them wildly, and then collapsed like an empty garment, and lay upon an engine similar to a bellows at its feet. Again the bellows sound roared, and again the figure leapt up and flung its arms to the sky. As I looked on, it did this many times, and I wondered at it, and was terrified.

"All along the brilliant avenue were divers interesting works and enterprises. I witnessed storefronts where one could obtain instruction in the martial arts of the Orient, and parlors in which members of the populace could cause their skin to be more tan, and useful places of exchange where notes drawn upon a local bank or issued by the state could be converted to cash money for a small fee. I saw eating establishments specializing in a kind of open-faced Italian pie, and offices of attorneys available to help those who had slipped and fallen, and clearly lighted venues in which the patrons could be marked with the latest and most intricate of tattoos, or could have previous, wrongly conceived tattoos removed, or (if they could not be removed) have them altered to different, less embarrassing tattoos. And everything was shining, and heavenly splendor was all around."

Brother Deserve's listeners sat in awe. Then an elder spoke. "Tell us, Brother, about the human beings of this city that is to be raised up here," he said. "In your vision, did you see men and women like ourselves?"

"Yes, human beings there were," Brother Deserve replied. "But very little like ourselves. Look at us—broomstick bodies, yellow with ague, some of us barely bones enough to hang our clothing on. No, the inhabitants of the city in my vision did not resemble us, for these were good-sized men and women, some as big around as four or five of us together! Their spreading forms showed the richness of the land, with flesh upon their limbs of vaster extent than we could possibly imagine, so that their very shirts and trousers could not completely cover buttocks, shins, and forearms, all plump and sleek as the butcher's dog!"

"Praise be!" the elder exclaimed, and the whole assembly agreed that the news rejoiced their hearts.

"I had a conversation as I made my way along the avenue," Brother Deserve continued, lost again in his memory. "In my right hand I held an object of about the size of a weaver's shuttle, and I lifted this object to my head, and from it a voice spoke unto me, and the voice said, 'Where are you?' And I replied, 'Here I am.' And the voice demanded, 'Where is "here"?' I fell on my face in unworthiness and said I truly did not know. The voice said, 'How long do you think it will take for you to get here?' I replied, 'You know this answer, not I.' Then the voice asked, 'Tell me what you see, and we will tell you how to go.' And I said, 'I see pits of endless flames of fire, and a sign that says BAR-B-Q BREAKFAST ALL DAY.' And the object made a noise like a frog peeping, and I heard no more."

Then the sky darkened, the canvas of the meeting tent ripped in half, and God Almighty spoke from the clouds. "BEWARE OF FALSE PROPHETS," God said. "THIS BROTHER DESERVE WHOM YOU HAVE LISTENED TO IS MISTAKEN. EVERYTHING HE SAID IS MADE UP BY HIM, AND WRONG. WHAT HE FORETOLD IS NEVER ACTUALLY GOING TO HAPPEN. TRUST IN ME, AND HAVE FAITH. KEEP DOING WHAT YOU ARE DOING. EVERYTHING IS GOING TO BE GREAT! HEAR ME!"

After the assembled brothers and sisters had recovered from their fright, they took Brother Deserve to the bank of the Wabash River and set him adrift in a small flat-bottomed boat with a cask of salt pork, a tin of pilot bread, and the latest real estate listings for parts downstream. He was not heard from again.

Enough to Make a Dog Laugh

I was sitting on a front porch in Helena, Montana, with my fourteen-year-old son on a hot summer afternoon when the smoke of nearby forest fires made the air even hotter. A black Labrador belonging to nobody we knew came walking along in a low, overheated mood. On a neighbor's lawn, a sprinkler was going. The dog saw it, bounded into the spray, and stayed there for a long while. Then he came out, shook himself a lot, and walked up onto the porch. He sat on his haunches looking at us. This was one happy dog. This dog owned happiness. Regarding us benevolently, his eyes had the fogginess of total bliss. Just sitting there, wet and dripping, he embodied the sound *ahhhhhhhhhhh*. My son and I agreed that we had never seen a human being as happy as that dog, and suddenly we became happy ourselves.

A dog's sense of smell is said to be ten thousand times better than a human's, and that's also how much better dogs are than humans at being happy. Human happiness is a shabby thing compared with a dog's. For eons, humans benefited from the canine gift for happiness and favored happy dogs, who thus passed along their happy genes, producing a species that is now besotted, almost deranged, with happiness. Of course, many other animals take pleasure in being alive—eagles soaring, otters skidding down slides, cows content to the point of smugness. But there's a selfishness to that happiness. Dog happiness always looks outward. To reach fullest expression, a dog's happiness has to be lived large and strewn around. The only thing that slows down a dog's happiness is if he can't infect you with it so you'll be happy together.

And dogs laugh! Not only do they laugh, they mean it, unlike such sarcastic types as monkeys, hyenas, and dolphins. (I know dolphins are friendly, but that high-pitched chuckle of theirs can wear on you.) A dog will laugh at anything. Hiding the ball, then pulling it out of your coat—hilarious! Watching you load the car before the vacation—a riot! Dogs are like an audience someone has already warmed up so that they laugh and voice their approval the minute the featured act (you) steps onto the stage. Dogs laugh even when they don't get the joke, which is often. But if you're laughing, it must be funny, and that's good enough for them.

To understand the sense of humor dogs have, it's useful to contrast it with that of their main pet competitor: cats. Cats do not really have a sense of humor. In its place, they cultivate a deep sense of the ironic. The detached, ironical pleasure cats take in watching and inflicting suffering is a horrid substitute for the hearty wholesomeness of dog laughter. And a cat never laughs out loud. The best that cats can muster is a sardonic smirk, an "I told you so" bared in their pointy incisors.

Dogs laugh just as hard when the joke is on them, but cats hate being the butt of laughter. One time my cat was asleep on the mantelpiece in the living room. In his sleep, he turned over, woke up, found himself lying on empty air, and began scrabbling frantically on the mantel with his front paws to keep from going down. Cartoon-like, he lost the struggle and dropped to the floor. I saw the whole thing and laughed my head off. Only the cat's dignity was injured, but he never forgave me, for the course of his half-hour memory span. He slunk around and shot me dirty looks and was really a bad sport about it, I thought. A dog would've made that same pratfall and hopped back on the mantel and done it again just for laughs.

Best of all, dogs live to go outdoors, where they find their funniest and timeliest material. They want to show you that running fast to nowhere in particular and then back, muddy and burr-covered, is such great comedy that you ought to join them in guffawing and jumping around with your tongue hanging out. They invite you to follow them to the railroad tracks and the run-over opossum that will be a good joke for them to roll in, or to the Canada geese on the baseball field, where a side-splitting chase scene will ensue. The bits are somehow even funnier because the dog is confident that you will love them as much as he does.

Dogs exult in the world itself. No matter if your neighborhood is interesting or not, your dog will want to go out in it. This is a godsend for human beings, most of whom would otherwise vanish into their screens. When I ramble around the part of New Jersey where I live, I see very few people on the sidewalks, and blue glows in many windows. The actual world has been abandoned for the virtual one— but not by dogs. They lobby for the world's reality and the unending comedic opportunities it provides. The only other humans I see on my rambles in the worst weather are the ones who have to walk their dogs. Dogs never stop showing us that gigantic happiness inheres in the world, waiting to be run to earth or sniffed on a tree.

Of Younger Days

When I was sixty-three, a cheeseburger at a diner on Fifty-Seventh Street cost $24.95, you could ride the Staten Island Ferry for free, and a kid could get a pretty decent college education for a quarter of a million dollars. Life was slower then, partly because of my newly acquired hip problem, but I did not know enough to appreciate the leisurely pace. I was always wanting to hurry up, to go faster and farther, to cross the street before the WALK signal ended. Now I wonder—why in the world was I in such a rush, back when I was sixty-three? Obviously, I did not want to get hit by a car, and there never seemed to be enough time to get across all twelve lanes of Queens Boulevard, the "Boulevard of Death." But now I often have trouble remembering what else seemed so almighty urgent to me back then.

During that never-to-be-repeated summer, I had just turned sixty-three when I began the hesitant, sweet, shy courtship of my first real girlfriend. My wife was furious, of course. It's poignant to think that today I've even forgotten her name—and my girlfriend's, too. The summer I was sixty-three was also when I had my second real girlfriend, and my fifth, and my eleventh. Looking back, and remembering how much I paid them, I wonder if they weren't prostitutes. But what did I know? I was just your typical gawky, self-conscious sixty-three-year-old, hormones going crazy. My voice had recently changed, from a high, piping tenor to a kind of guttural, gurgling rasp. My body was changing, too, and I became very aware of and embarrassed by the large breasts I had developed. So much seemed new and unfamiliar when I was sixty-three.

That enchanted summer was all about the music. I gave myself over entirely to the many songs I heard everywhere—in elevators, on SiriusXM, in shopping malls, in my periodontist's office—as they created a powerful soundtrack for my days and nights. Even today, when I hear a certain lyric from that lost summer of however long ago, and Katy Perry sings that she's "comin' at you like a [something?] horse," bittersweet tears fill my eyes. How could anything so lovely be so fleeting? The radiance has fled, but to where? Looking back, I regret that I did not go to more concerts, choosing instead just to hum the tunes while Dr. Tonnelli packed cotton under my lip before the gum augmentation. And where did those concerts take place, anyway, and what were the names of the people or the bands (if they were bands) I listened to? Now I'll never know unless I look them up.

The summer I was sixty-three was also when I went to San Francisco. One morning, I just dropped everything, said goodbye to everybody I could get in touch with, and flew out there in a middle seat in economy. San Francisco was different then, in the early sixties—my early sixties, that is. I look at the wild haircut I had back then and I have to laugh! And where in the world did I get those pants? Yes, I am still wearing them right now, but where did I get them? At the Short Hills Mall, I think. In San Francisco, I did a lot of experimenting with drugs, mainly because I had problems getting my prescription for blood-pressure medication renewed on a weekend. I may have permanently messed up my DNA, but it was worth it. You take all kinds of risks when you're younger, and sixty-three. You think you're immortal.

If some genie granted me the power to reverse time and meet up with my naïve sixty-three-year-old self, what advice would I give him? I might say, "Sixty-three-year-old, hang on tightly to experience while it's in your grasp, especially the sales slips. And don't be afraid to try new outfits, which are what you'll later need the sales slips for. Dump your oil stocks, because the price of oil is going to come down. But, mainly, younger self—*live!* The mysterious, glorious, ineffable sweetness of being sixty-three will come to you only once on this earth."

But then my sixty-three-year-old self would say back to me, "Yes, yes, I know. But tell me more about the price of oil. Will it go below fifty dollars a barrel? And what horse should I bet in the Belmont? And what odds should I give?"

That would probably hurt my feelings, because I'm imparting hard-won, sixty-four-year-old life advice here. So I would then knee my sixty-three-year-old self in the groin, and, when he (I) bent over, give him (me) an uppercut with both fists. Then he (I) would really understand what it means to be sixty-three.

Confab

Sit down and talk with your kids about it. If you don't think you have time in your family's busy schedule, *make* time to talk about it. Your kids should hear about it from you, as soon as is convenient, in a setting that's familiar and unthreatening. Chances are, they know about it already, and will be grateful to you for dealing with it openly.

The first time we talked about it with our kids, I followed the advice I'm giving you now. Marjorie and I gathered them together after supper and told them that we needed to talk about something very important. Then we all sat down around the kitchen table—and I can't stress too strongly how important it is to sit down. Some of the kids kept wanting to stand up, but we kept telling them to sit down. Then, once we were all seated, we began to talk about it. The conversation was forthright, frank, measured, and equal in seriousness to what we were talking about.

When we were finished, we asked the kids if they had any questions or concerns. Our second son, Miles, got a thoughtful look on his face, and posed a question that I remember to this day. "Mom, Dad," he said, with some hesitation. "Did you know that Alfred Hitchcock had his navel surgically removed?"

Are we always listening as closely as we should be when our kids ask us questions? If Marjorie and I had not talked candidly with our kids that day, Miles's meaningful question probably would not have come up. Neither of us had ever heard that particular "fact" about Alfred Hitchcock, so at first we could not be of much help. But we assured Miles that we admired the critical thinking he had used to arrive at his question. His honest inquisitiveness then inspired his sister June, a kindergartner, to ask a follow-up.

"If a little bee played baseball," June inquired, "would he need his whole body just to carry the ball?"

Springboarding off June's contribution, Jason, age eight, then introduced a tangential line of questioning that put the discussion into deeper perspective. "Okay, Billy Nolan told me this," Jason began. "Is it true that in an average lifetime an average person eats six spiders in their sleep?"

Marjorie and I have taught our children that every question is equally valid—i.e., there is no such thing as a "wrong" question. Naturally, when we've been talking about a subject as full of implications as the subject of our family conference that evening, every question must be weighed respectfully and with due reflection. We now had three topics for further looking into:

1. The Hitchcock-navel question.
2. Bees and baseball.
3. Spiders being eaten, etc.

Each of these had the potential to open a new angle on the important exchange of ideas between our children and ourselves which had begun when we all sat down around the table. Quite honestly, I thought we now had plenty to deal with. Sadik, however, added an interesting sidelight when he asked whether it was possible to make lasagna out of different kinds of ice cream, so I put "Lasagna/ice cream?" as No. 4 on our list.

Kids take in so much more than we give them credit for. The wheels in their heads are always turning. As proof of that, Jaden, who's five, raised his hand. When Marjorie encouraged him to say what was on his mind, he shyly asked us to guess which part of his nose he had just picked. I was not sure where that question fit on the list I already had, so I started a new list, "Jaden's nose: Which part picked?" and told him that we would deal with his question soon.

Perhaps apropos of June's question about the bee, her sister, Mabel, who will be four next month, wondered out loud whether dinosaurs had butts. I admitted I did not see what that had to do with the subject of our family confab, and I pressed, gently, for the relevance of Mabel's ask. By way of clarification, she offered that Tyler (her older brother, age seven) had said he could kick a dinosaur's butt, and she, Mabel, did not know if dinosaurs *had* butts. Where to put that question on the lists? I told Mabel that I was writing it on the first list, but in fact I only pretended to.

The twins, Dashiell and Mikey, who are ten and very into tech things, brought up a concern with a limited but real connection to what we were exploring. They asked if Marjorie or I knew what the loudest-decibel burp of all time was. We've never pretended to be informed about everything, and as it happened we did not have that particular information. Instead we tried, as we've been trained, to hear the question *behind* the question that the child is asking. After providing a sensitive-listening moment in which Dash and Mikey could expand on this, we discovered that the real question behind the question also had to do with the loudest-decibel burp of all time. Turning to Gus, age twelve, we let him offer some guidance, which he kind of did by asking if we knew that somebody once made a replica of the *Mona Lisa* entirely out of burnt toast.

I have changed all the children's names in order to protect their privacy. That is, after ill-advisedly using their actual names in this essay, I have changed their names in real life. Their well-being must always come first. Sitting down to talk with them has become a weekly ritual, which they seem to value highly even though it drove Marjorie crazy several months ago and she ran off with an events planner who has no children. Well-meaning friends say that perhaps what we talked about should not have been talked about to begin with. That is nonsense. You have to talk about it, as an overwhelming percentage of Americans agree. The only mistake bigger than not talking about it is talking about it (or anything else) without first sitting down.

Still Looking

> Its gripping, foot-on-the-gas plot touches on the fall of the Berlin Wall, stolen Stasi files and a missing thermonuclear warhead.
>
> —From a book review in *The New York Times*

A: It was right here a minute ago.

B: Think back. What were you doing when you saw it last?

A: I remember the Berlin Wall was falling, I had just got up to put the wash in the dryer, and it was on the coffee table, in its wood-and-molybdenum caddy. I drove down to the Laundro, shot several policemen, and ran over a fruit seller. Yes, I specifically remember the oranges rolling all over the street in my rearview mirror. And when I finally got back home it was gone.

B: Have you looked behind the refrigerator?

A: Of course. That's the first place I thought of.

B: So you must have put it somewhere. What did you do after the Laundromat?

A: I went out to get a pack of smokes at the corner. I noticed five helicopters following me, and I realized that they were homing in on a tracking device that somebody had sewn into my clothes. I started to run, shedding my shirt, my shoes, my socks, and my trousers. As I got to the upper level of the Oberbaum Bridge, I guessed that the transmitter must be in my boxer shorts, so I took them off, too, and threw them into the Spree just as the missiles hit them and blew them up. When I got home, I was exhausted and took a short nap.

B: I know where it must be! Did you leave it plugged into the charger?

A: It doesn't need a charger. It uses fission first, and then fusion.

B: Do you suppose the cleaning people might have done something with it?

A: (*Inaudible.*)

C: I was the girlfriend of the two individuals whose dialogue, taken from surveillance, is transcribed above. The three of us lived in a flat, which is what they call an apartment in Germany. I would have to hear the actual tape to know which of the speakers is A and which is B. They were not the ones who stole the Stasi files—that was me. I had a reusable shopping bag with a picture of Christa Wolf on it, in which I smuggled the files out of Stasi headquarters. I took hundreds and hundreds. Most were regular rat tail files, but there were also plenty of nail files, cuticle files, and two-handed carpentry files. I also stole a lot of rasps, but somehow no one ever cared about those.

When the thermonuclear warhead turned up missing, we were all frantic, of course. My "friends"—I guess that's the correct term—did not want to go to the police, for obvious reasons, but I insisted. As it happened, I went alone. A woman detective took down my description of the lost object. I told her it was about so big around, holding my arms in a circle, which she measured with forensic calipers, and about this long, holding my hands a certain distance apart, which she also measured. I told her it was flat at one end and came to a cone-like point at the other. I said, "It's a thermonuclear warhead, for God's sake!" She asked me to be more specific, and when I couldn't she brought in the department's sketch artist, who was able to produce a creditable rendering based on what I told him.

We are all aware of how fussy the Germans can be. Here is where things become gripping and foot-on-the-gas. When I looked more closely at the sketch, I saw that the artist had drawn the chief inspector of police. The likeness was uncanny and unmistakable. Yet all of us—the artist, the woman detective, and myself—had taken the drawing to be a depiction of the object that I had described. Could it be that the missing thermonuclear warhead and the chief inspector were one and the same?

I had to find out more.

✷✷✷

What you have been reading is only a simulation. If it were an actual novel, it would be too much for the average human tolerance and nobody would still be alive. Fortunately, we can prepare for this grim possibility without exposing ourselves to unnecessary risk. The rules are simple: First, never read a novel that involves a missing thermonuclear warhead. If, for some reason, you do find yourself in the middle of such a novel, go to the nearest civil defense shelter or hazmat-qualified book group. They will know what to do.

German translation:
WAS SIE GELESEN HABEN IST NUR EINE SIMU-LIERUNG! WENN ES SICH UM EINEN ROMAN

HANDELN WÜRDE, WÄRE DIES ZU VIEL FÜR DIE DURCHSCHNITTLICHE MENSCHLICHE TOLERANZ UND NIEMAND WÜRDE ÜBERLEBEN. GLÜCKLI-CHERWEISE KÖNNEN WIR UNS FÜR DIESE DÜSTERE MÖGLICHKEIT VORBEREITEN OHNE UNS DEN UN-NÖTIGEN RISIKEN ZU STELLEN. DIE REGELN SIND SIMPLE: ERSTENS, LESE NIEMALS EINEN ROMAN—

(*A refrigerator door opens, followed by a flash brighter than ten thousand suns; mushroom cloud.*)

The Rise of Artificial Unintelligence

Computers may one day be able to reason exactly as humans do, but will they ever be as dumb? I had always thought that was impossible. Now, however, I'm not so sure. The other day, I was in Penn Station on my way home from work. A team of scientists had set up a table with a laptop running the latest pattern-recognition software, and they were asking passersby to suggest questions for the computer. With twenty minutes on my hands, I asked it to find the best place for me to sit while waiting for my train. The word "processing" blinked on the screen for a minute or so. Then a photo appeared, with an "X" and a flashing arrow marking the spot. I looked more closely. The place the computer had indicated was nearby, on a busy stairway, directly beneath a sign that said DO NOT SIT ON STAIRS— the very spot I often choose myself!

A bit stunned, I went and rested there, causing the usual bottleneck of hurrying commuters, some of whom tripped over me. A computer as witless as I am—how can we maintain our irreducible humanity in the face of that?

Maybe it was just a fluke. Reassuring myself that the machine could never duplicate such a lucky hit, I went back and asked the computer, by way of the scientists, if it thought I should put novelty reindeer antlers on my car. This time, the reply came instantly: a simple "Yes." I looked at the screen, impressed. Then, knocking me even flatter, it followed up with "And a bumper sticker that says I ROLLER-SKATE—DEAL WITH IT!" I don't roller-skate, but I had to admit that I admired the statement's attitude. Again, the computer was eerily right.

The scientists, who were young guys of the sort you would expect, talked among themselves in low, smug voices. I hung around, pretending to look at my phone, and eavesdropped. Oh, how pleased these guys were with the way their new program had performed! Already that evening, the computer had forgotten to call home and tell its "wife"— another computer, apparently—that it would be late, and then had inadvertently sent "her" embarrassing flirtatious emails intended for another computer at the office. Can everything I do, everything I *am*, be translated so easily into code? I felt myself descending further into despair.

No, damn it! *I am a human being!* Our species does poorly thought-out things, and we must not take a backseat to any machine on that. Remember when I saw Bev at the Shelbys' New Year's Eve party and blurted out, in front of everybody, "Bev, how fabulous! You're pregnant!" when she had only put on a lot of weight? I defy any mere mass of circuitry to duplicate this deeply human feat. As I recalled the horror on Bev's face, and on everybody else's, my entire body contorted in a wince of shame and—I'll be honest—a certain species-specific pride. Top that, techno-wizards! Other un-smart stunts came back to me: No computer will ever amass enough mainframe cluelessness to cut a big patch from the pair of blue jeans that it is mending rather than from the old blue jeans that it uses for patches. Nor will it ever finish filling out its income tax return and then mail it, along with the check for the IRS, to a distant relative it hasn't seen in years. You need to be a living, breathing, flesh-and-blood creature to achieve such things.

I calmed myself down, proceeded to the platform, got on the wrong train, and did not notice my mistake until Trenton. The train back to Penn Station would not leave for another hour and a half. I never expect to be as smart as a computer, but, by God, I can be dumber. A hard rain began to fall, and I left the station so I could practice not knowing enough to come in out of it.

UPDATE: The consequences of the events related above are so well-known as not to need a detailed repetition here. Preliminary reconstruction of the disaster has revealed the outline of what occurred. Evidently, the computer that the subject confronted in Penn Station tracked him, by GPS signal, to Trenton. When it received an indication that he had foolishly exited into the rain, the computer, not to be outdone (or, to use tech jargon, "outdumbed"), distracted its scientist handlers with complicated prompts that caused them to carry it into the storm, which had by then settled over the entire East Coast. A sudden drowning in the downpour not only destroyed the computer but somehow led to a mass suicide spasm among linked programs, with thousands of computers and other devices ruining themselves in coffee spills, dog bowl plunges, hot tub dunkings, and so on. In the wake of these occurrences, all Artificial Stupidity (AS) research has been halted, pending investigation.

The Disturbing Case of the Dead Witch

I live in what my wife and I like to think of as a safe neighborhood. Recently, however, at a house just up the street, I have noticed disturbing evidence of possible criminal activity, or, at the very least, a violation of local zoning laws. What stopped me short one morning as I was walking our dog was the sight of a "human" corpse smashed up against the front of this house. I put the word in quotation marks because I'm not quite sure to what category the poor dead creature belongs.

It was as flat as a pancake and had evidently hit the house at a high rate of speed. To me, it appeared to be a witch. Among the seasonal decorations at the house—a plastic pumpkin, a sheaf of Indian corn, a silhouette of a black cat arching its back—this grisly, flattened body, with a witch's hat still in place and a broom also stuck to the siding, sent a shudder of revulsion mixed with pity down my spine. One could picture the accident all too clearly. A young witch, hardly more than a child, is flying too fast on her broom, then: *crash!* The little arms outstretched on either side, the green fingers spread in a hopeless last-minute attempt to soften the impact, were enough to break your heart.

The negligence of the homeowners was all the more shocking because they happened to have a cemetery in the front yard. Small gray plastic tombstones announced that

Frankenstein's monster, Dracula, and the Wolf Man were all interred there. Surely it would not be too much to hope that the unlucky little witch be given a decent burial as well, even if she was not a celebrity.

One of the mourners who was visiting the cemetery, a lanky young fellow who wore a hockey mask and carried a chainsaw, stood unmoving, as if in shock, beside the Wolf Man's grave. "Did you know him?" I asked quietly. The grief-stricken fellow did not reply.

A troubling detail about the grave of Dracula caught my eye. It was a skeletal arm reaching out of the well-manicured lawn. If Dracula had in fact been buried alive, as the skeleton arm seemed to suggest, that made a certain amount of unfortunate sense; when you spend your days lying in a coffin, you do run the risk of this kind of mix-up. But how did no one see the arm waving in the air, after it had laboriously burst through the sod? And why was it ignored, waving and waving, ever more slowly, until death finally arrived, blessedly, for the supposedly deathless vampire? Rigor mortis then set in, followed by weeks and months of rot and decay and scavenging by local animals, until the bones of the arm were all that remained. What kind of clueless homeowners could fail to notice such a hideous process taking place on their own front lawn?

Enough was enough. I walked to the front door and rang the bell. A handsome, smiling couple in late middle age answered. We got to talking. And that, in short, is how I happened to run for and be elected to the Parsippany school board.

If the story had ended there, all would have been well. But, sadly, a sequel occurred to darken that happy outcome.

It started out quite innocently. As the school board president, I proposed a new policy mandating that only healthy snacks be given to trick-or-treaters. The ordinance was duly voted upon and passed, and I offered to keep an eye open for any violators. Going around the neighborhood and looking in windows, I noticed that the Kremser family seemed to have some snack-size boxes of Milk Duds ready in a wooden salad bowl by the door. I went around to the back and met Mr. and Mrs. Kremser coming in from the garage. I told them, very politely, that the treats I had observed in their front hall were not allowed. Overreacting, Mr. Kremser began to shout and turn red in the face. In a matter of seconds, he had a heart attack and dropped dead.

Of course I felt terrible. I thought that the very least I could do was offer to defray some of the funeral costs, and suggested to my helpful neighbors with the front yard cemetery that we give Mr. Kremser a plot there. They proceeded to inform me that *it was not a real cemetery* (italics mine). Now, I had wondered why the mourner with the chainsaw remained in the exact same position for hours and even weeks without leaving for food and other necessities, but I had not wanted to pry, and my neighbors did not go out of their way to correct any mistaken impression I might have had.

I'm sure there's a lesson somewhere in all this. Building community takes patience, time, and (sometimes) a regrettable loss of life. But we also have a double standard. The fact remains that a long-dead, decaying young witch is still plastered against my neighbors' house. Let's try a little thought experiment:

Would the corpse of a full-grown warlock, a male individual with some power and influence, be subjected to such indignity if he happened to be flying on a much larger broom and ended up smashing into the wall of someone's house? I think we can all agree that the answer is obvious.

Incident Review

After watching a double feature of *Sully* and *Star Trek Beyond*:

From the proceedings of the National Transportation Safety Board:

Report on the Flight of the Starship *Enterprise* Through the Nebula to Rescue a Stranded Crew on a Mystery Planet; the Subsequent Crash; and the Actions of the Crew of the *Enterprise*, Up to and Including Its Return to Yorktown, the Resupply Planet. Submitted to the United States Congress and the Rulers of the Federation.

Summary of events leading up to the incident:

On January 14, at 10:55 a.m., the Starship *Enterprise* took off from LaGuardia Airport, New York City, on a flight to the nebula. Three minutes and four seconds after takeoff, geese were struck, and Krall, a lizard-type alien, after crashing his own spacecraft into the *Enterprise*, went running around inside shooting at crew members with some kind of ray gun and looking for an ancient relic that would give him the power to dematerialize things.

At 11:03 a.m., Captain James T. Kirk of the *Enterprise* made a Mayday call to the tower at LaGuardia and was advised to return to the airport, with emergency vehicles standing by.

At 11:04.57 a.m., Captain Kirk radioed the tower and explained about the lizard alien and said he did not think he could get to LaGuardia under the circumstances. Tower advised him to try Teterboro Airport, in Teterboro, New Jersey, or Liberty International Airport, in Newark.

At 11:06.17 a.m., after consulting with Commander Spock and getting into a fistfight with Krall, Captain Kirk informed the tower that, instead of landing at Newark or Teterboro, he was going to try to head for the nebula.

At 11:12.03 a.m., the tower lost radio contact with the *Enterprise*.

From the transcript of the inquest:

FIRST COMMISSIONER: Captain Kirk, I am wondering why you did not simply return to LaGuardia Airport at the very beginning of the incident.

CAPTAIN KIRK: I made the best decision I could at the time. Also, Krall was making these horrible breathing noises. (*Imitates the noises.*)

SECOND COMMISSIONER: Captain, we'd like to play for you a video from our flight simulator, demonstrating that the *Enterprise* could have returned to LaGuardia Airport safely, had you followed tower's advisement to do so. Can we play the video, please? As you see, here our simulator pilots are taking off . . . Now they hit the geese . . . Now Krall crashes into the *Enterprise* . . . Now he shoots at crew members with his ray gun . . . Here he is holding you up against the cockpit wall with his massive claw . . . Here the *Enterprise* begins to turn . . . And here it lands safely at LaGuardia Airport.

CAPTAIN KIRK: With all due respect—

THIRD COMMISSIONER: Excuse me, but I wish to follow up with further simulator-test data that pertains to events on the so-called mystery planet. Again, the simulator suggests that your decisions were ill-considered. Here we see Captain Kirk discover a motorcycle in a wrecked starship . . . Here we see him ride around among Krall's guards in order to allow his crew to escape . . . Here the motorcycle begins to turn . . . And here it enters a wormhole and lands safely at LaGuardia Airport.

CAPTAIN KIRK: If I may—

FIRST COMMISSIONER: We request that you kindly hold your comments until we have shown all the data. The next and, frankly, most troubling simulator test shows what appears to be a serious lapse in judgment. Here you are on Yorktown, the supply planet, chasing Krall, who has the ancient artifact and intends to dematerialize everybody with it. Now you and Krall begin another fistfight . . . He falls through a space hatch and is sucked into deep space . . . You begin to fall through the space hatch yourself . . . Mr. Spock and Bones come flying into the space hatch in a little spaceship . . . They rescue you . . . And, the next thing we see, you and your fellow crew members are drinking and celebrating in a lounge.

CAPTAIN KIRK: In this case, the simulator has reproduced exactly what did, in fact, occur, so I don't understand your question.

SECOND COMMISSIONER: After Spock and Bones rescued you, why did you not order them to return safely to LaGuardia Airport?

FIRST COMMISSIONER: Do you have something against LaGuardia Airport, Captain?

CAPTAIN KIRK: No, Madame Commissioner, I do not. Although it is a third-galaxy airport and its runways are too short, I will make use of it or any other airport I am ordered to use, because I am a starship captain, as was my father before me. What I do object to is judgment without informed deliberation. Our mission to the mystery planet was successful. I came to terms with the ghost of my father. Spock was able to get back together with Uhuru. The universe did not get dematerialized. Insurance will pay for a new *Enterprise*, which, frankly, needed replacing. I stand by every decision that I made. (*Spontaneous applause.*)

THIRD COMMISSIONER: Captain Kirk, after much discussion among ourselves, we, the members of the National Transportation Safety Board, have decided that you performed your duties in an exemplary fashion. You are free to go, with our heartfelt thanks.

FIRST COMMISSIONER: But, before you leave, will you do us one favor?

CAPTAIN KIRK: What is that?

FIRST COMMISSIONER: Will you please just go out to LaGuardia Airport and at least take a look around? It's really not that bad. There's an Artichoke Pizza there now. For us?

(*Suddenly the face of Krall, hideously huge, appears on the screen behind the commissioners. Panic, bystanders screaming.*)

FACE OF KRALL: Splendid, splendid! (*Laughs maniacally.*)

Why Mummies?

Nowadays, when I tell prospective employers to consider mummies, the other undead temp option, I am met with blank stares. How is it that in just a few short years we've forgotten about our old reliable standbys, the mummies? Simple: We live in the golden age of zombies.

I often remind personnel directors at competitive companies that mummies work 80 percent cheaper than zombies. Mummies are also slightly more articulate, and they are easier to deal with if they become enraged. If a mummy starts to chase you, merely pull on a loose end of one of his bandages and spin him like a top, unwinding him until he collapses in a pile of bones. Unlike zombies, 97 percent of mummies are not unionized, and some have even been known to threaten union organizers with bloody butcher knives.

Antigrowth forces sometimes fault us for leasing out mummies to serve as the operators of giant construction cranes. But all our mummies are legally bonded and receive up to two days of refresher training every third year, as is required by law. Mummies are allowed to work more than eight hours in a single shift. And here's another dollar saver: they are not eligible for overtime pay, because of laws involving forfeiture of certain privileges resulting from having escaped (in many cases) from state-funded universities or museums.

Public safety advocates have cited isolated incidents in which a mummy became upset while operating a giant construction crane. Remember, these operators are the mummified remains of the same people who built the pyramids. We think they know a little bit about building things!

It is true that once or twice a giant construction crane has gotten away from the mummy who was operating it. I'm sure we've all seen the videos, and the reports from the hospitals and the morgues, and the sensationalized pictures of the crushed orphanage (the one that was crushed in both incidents, last year and the previous year). Apparently, a Great Dane has been implicated in the event, along with a group of meddling teenagers who were investigating mysterious noises in a haunted mansion and somehow opened the sarcophagus in which the mummy in question, Amenhotep, was resting after a long shift working the giant construction crane. Experts cited lack of sleep as a cause of the accident, and neither the mummy nor our firm was convicted of the main charges, though he was sentenced to perform thirty hours of community service. (While performing his community service, Amenhotep did briefly chase a local TV reporter with a bloody butcher knife.)

Now, regarding the other incident: First, you must remember how hard it is to operate the controls of a giant construction crane when one's embalmed hands are swathed in ancient linen wrappings impregnated with tar-based mummifying substances. The mummy's fine motor skills are impaired, and this leads to frustration on the part of the mummy, who, after all, was only human. A mummy in this situation is liable to "act out," making muffled groaning noises and moving about erratically. The crane then begins to swing wildly, smashing into neighboring skyscrapers. This upsets the mummy further, and he groans more loudly. So far, however, no real damage has been done.

In the incident I'm referring to, the more serious problems began when the mummy took a bloody butcher knife and began to attack the controls of the giant construction crane. The bloody butcher knife is often a mummy's default response, and sometimes we must work around it, inconvenient (and occasionally dangerous) as it may be. All our mummies know the rule "Use words, not bloody butcher knives," because we drum it into them as part of the training. But in panic situations it's not always foolproof. Every thought leaves the mummies' brains, which probably aren't in their skulls anyway, having been removed and mummified separately and put in amphorae.

All this may seem to outweigh the arguments for why you should hire one of the mummies represented by our firm. But remember: Mummies rarely feed on human flesh, while zombies stuff themselves with it. So why is there all this buzz about zombies? (And we don't mean the swarms of blue-bottle flies attracted by their putrefaction.) More is going on here than meets the eye falling out of its socket and dangling by the optic nerve. Look no further than K Street, in Washington, D.C., and the multimillion-dollar lobbying firms that are clustered there. Better yet, ask Ms. Jane Austen, who featured zombies in all her exquisitely wrought nineteenth-century comedies of manners. Research has revealed that supporters of mummies begged her time and again to give a mummy even a tiny role in *Pride and Prejudice and Zombies*, but she refused. Now it is known that Ms. Jane Austen was in the pocket of the zombie lobby up to her eyebrows.

Savvy businesspeople understand that dirt cheap mummies mean bigger paydays for our neighbors and for our communities. Even if you are a job creator who has been bitten and turned into a zombie yourself, that's okay, as long as you remain on the other side of the electrified steel barricade. We will be happy to provide the mummy or mummies who are right for you.

Goodbye, My Funding

I was walking down the street one afternoon, when I suddenly lost funding. At first, I couldn't identify what the strange feeling was—a sort of lightness in the right rear pocket, where I kept my wallet, and a chest-tightening deficiency of balance, and a sensation as if all the rubber bands around my bankroll had been cut. Afterward, I learned that adult-onset funding loss often presents in this fashion, but at the time I had no idea what was happening, and I was concerned.

Loss of funding (LOF) afflicts more than 92 percent of the population. It can strike at any moment, often with little warning. Researchers have recently unlocked some of the biophysical secrets of this scourge. Apparently, when funding loss occurs, a flow of electronic transfers is interrupted, causing a lack of distribution to fund-sensitive receptor cells in the brain. Within ninety seconds, these cells begin to suffer stresses; in another three minutes, the cerebral cortex goes totally dead. If you do not get to a high-wealth prospect or a ranking office bureaucrat in time, the damage can be irreversible. Many people who lose funding are never the same. Others are sometimes able to return to normal lives.

The invisible force we now know as funding was discovered in the early twentieth century by railway workers digging a tunnel in France. One of the workmen's shovels struck something huge and ineffable, and there it was. Scientists then required decades to isolate it, describe it, and give it the name it has today, which is based on the English word for money. Even now, many of us may not realize that money and funding share a common ancestry. Were it not for funding, there would be no life on Earth, or no life as we know it. Recently, some scientists who had been funded to study single-cell life-forms in volcanic cracks in Earth's crust at the bottom of the Pacific Ocean discovered that these bacteria themselves depend on funding. Tracing their wider circulation throughout the planet's systems, the scientists found that certain ocean-vent bacteria make regular appearances in northwestern Canada, presumably to solicit Robert Smith. Afterward, the stay-at-home worker bacteria "reimburse" their traveling reps with mitochondrial donations when they return to the ocean bottom. Thus, the whole global ecosphere is connected by an intricate web of funding.

For me, loss of funding has been especially painful, because not only am I used to being funded, I also fund. In fact, many recipients have told me that no funder funds like I fund. I have even been called the Fundin' Fool. To have to disappoint those people seeking funding has been heartbreaking. I take their applications, so carefully prepared by well-funded grant-writing specialists, and tear the pages into tiny pieces before the would-be fundees' eyes. Then I watch them exhibit the same symptoms that came over me—death, basically, but the kind of death that keeps you looking outwardly the same while you're all rotted inside.

Fortunately, help is on the way. If you feel that you have been defunded, there's a number you can call. Also, exciting new possibilities may exist in space. Today, a NASA satellite is traveling the outermost reaches of our galaxy in search of additional funding. Excitement ran high last year, when funds were observed on a flyby over Mars, but they turned out to be only Martian rocks. It is still highly probable that funding exists on one of the trillions of objects out there in space. Promising schemes have been proposed to extract funding from cosmic rays using a technology that traps the rays in a matrix of informal, low-key private luncheons. However, such ideas still remain at the event-planning stage.

I know it's too late for me. My own beloved funding will never come back. If your funding up and leaves the way mine did, nothing you can say or do will change its mind. For a while, hoping against all reason, I held on to some of the toiletries that my funding had left in the bathroom. Finally, that got too sad, so I gave them to an organization that provides personal-care items to lesser fundings that do not have them. What still tears me apart is thinking of my funding with someone else. In March, I caught a glimpse of my funding in mid-town, getting into a black SUV with a bearded man. My funding saw me, too—I could tell by the wistfulness of its expression, and its faint, fiscally poignant smile. My former funding is one classy amount of funding, I'll say that. And let's not be coy. It's some of the top funding available anywhere, by which I mean in the neighborhood of thirty-seven Gs. Goodbye, my funding. May you always be happy. May your new love never forget what a treasure he has. You still possess my never-to-be-funded-again heart.

Victor Laszlo's Blog

> Victor Laszlo is on that plane!
> —Captain Renault, in *Casablanca*

December 5, 10:15 p.m. Just took off from Morocco. If you're wondering why I haven't posted for a few weeks, it's because I ran into some difficulties here. So great to be finally leaving! Also great to be on a plane with free Wi-Fi. It's rare to get that on one of these old prop jobs. I won't go into the long story of how Mrs. Laszlo and I were finally cleared to go, but, basically, an old friend of hers who happens to run a bar came up with some "letters of transit," etc., etc. German bureaucracy plus French incompetence—the old story. I'll be glad when we land at Lisbon.

December 6. So here we are in Portugal! I found a big stack of newspapers waiting in our (rather so-so) hotel room. This morning I sat right down and went through them to find out what jaw-dropping things Hitler said and/or did recently. Where do I even begin? The man has all the emotional depth of a coat of varnish. (That is actually something I thought of back when we were in Casablanca, but I haven't had a chance to use it until now.)

December 8. I didn't have time to post yesterday, because Mrs. Laszlo was suffering from some kind of problem. She was listless and depressed. Probably she drank some of that buggy Casablanca water. I drink only bottled myself.

Heard a good remark about Hitler yesterday. When it comes time for him to build the Führer's Official Library, it will probably be all marble and glitz and swastikas and gilt—with only one book! (The point, of course, is that he does not read books. Probably he hasn't even read his own!)

Through humor we will prevail in our struggle.

December 9. This morning I sat down to write my inspirational radio address to the members of the underground movement in my country. The first step is to figure out what country I am from. I think it's Hungary or Czechoslovakia or one of those. I'll have to do some research on that. When I tried to come up with stirring words to lift the human soul in the face of brutal tyranny and violence, I got kind of stuck. Then I had a brilliant idea—write the speech in my blog voice! I'm much more informal and relaxed on my blog. After that, the words just flowed.

December 10. Mrs. Laszlo still does not seem to be her old self—I'm not sure why. Last night in her sleep, she kept saying something like "Looking at you kids" over and over. Once, I heard her say, distinctly, "Here's looking at Yul, kid!" Who could that be? Yul Brynner? How does she know him? Then she woke up, saw me, and burst into tears.

December 11. Can you believe the latest from Hitler? I'm almost beyond being shocked at anything he does. I will say this as an established fact: Hitler is unqualified to be Führer.

He is a disgrace to the Führer-ship and should resign. If he refuses, we must resist by . . . by simply resisting. As a matter of fact, I'm resisting right now, out on the hotel veranda.

December 15. Skipped my blog for a while because I took a few days just for myself and did nothing! Not one thing! Fighting fascism has taken a lot out of me, and I deserved a break. Meanwhile, the fellow from Casablanca, the one who owns (or owned) the bar (apparently he sold it to the guy with the fez?), showed up here suddenly. It seems that he and that French captain caught a later flight. The (ex-) bar owner and Mrs. Laszlo assured me that they needed a room to themselves in a separate hotel in order to treat her condition.

December 16. Got back into the fray by going around singing "La Marseillaise" in various public places, to show defiance. And I've partnered with a local comedian who does a screamingly funny Hitler impersonation. If we can just achieve a bit wider notice, the battle for Europe is as good as won.

The British Museum of Your Stuff

From an exhibition on display in the British Museum's Permanent and Non-Returnable Collection of American Antiquities and Near-Antiquities:

Object 1-A: Rawlings baseball glove, circa 1959. While on a collecting trip in search of artifacts in a remote part of the American interior known as Ohio, William Fitzmorris, fifth Earl of Litchfield, discovered this mint condition example of a "ball mitt" lying in plain sight just inside the back door of a single-family home. Shipped with a crate of similar acquisitions, the item was cataloged and entered irretrievably into the museum's holdings in 1960.

Object 1-B: Schwinn "Roadmaster" boy's bicycle, bright blue with white detailing, circa 1962. This museum-quality velocipede of American manufacture was stumbled upon by Sir Chauncey Peakes, KBE, as he was studying small-village bicycle racks in search of clues to the indigenous cultures left unlocked. Finding the rare two-wheeler propped negligently against a tree, Sir Chauncey quickly stowed it in the back of his archeologist's van and airfreighted it to London, so that it would not fall into the hands of the French.

Object 1-C: Baseball card issued by Topps Bubble Gum Company (Woody Held, Cleveland Indians shortstop),

1964. In the course of a hot and sweaty midsummer dig in a hard-to-reach Ohio dwelling-place closet while the inhabitants were carelessly out, Martin Smythe, of the museum's near-antiquities staff, spotted this priceless treasure and plucked it up straightaway. Chain of continuous possession being impossible to establish, the ownership of the object has reverted firmly and decisively to the museum.

Object 1-D: The Enderbee Stereo. This superb example of an American stereo was discovered in a crudely furnished dormitory room during winter break in 1971 by Arturo St. Ides, the tenth Lord Enderbee, while on an international expedition looking for things that belonged to other people. In the interest of science and the preservation of human heritage, he let us purchase it rather than disposing of it with a dealer in hot goods, where it would be lost. The Enderbee Stereo, one of the finest works of that important period, is now wholly owned by us.

Object 2-A: Of particular interest is this 1975 Ford Maverick automobile, which Cecil Fisk-Weatherford Jones, antiquarian and museum trustee, came upon and hot-wired in a supermarket car park in one of the New England states circa 1979. Having gutted this remarkable find for parts, each of which told a story about bygone times, Fisk-Weatherford Jones arranged for the museum to acquire the remainder. The cinder blocks supporting each corner are contemporary to the period.

Objects 3-B and 3-C: Dame Helen Gothschild, while on a collecting trip in the American Rocky Mountains, sensed the presence of these lightweight hiking boots inside a poorly secured storage locker used by patrons of Big Sky

Resort, near Butte, Montana, and painstakingly made off with them. The original owner, who, having stowed the boots while he skied with rental boots and skis, had to return home in his stocking feet—too bad. Boots of this type are no longer manufactured, and the museum intends never to part with these, whether the original owner produces the sales slip and notarized photographs of himself wearing the boots, or not.

Object 3-E: Wallet, leather, circa 2017. A team of museum experts obtained this almost new wallet by jostling a tourist on a Nevsky Prospekt trolleybus in St. Petersburg, Russia, and relieving him of it—tough cheese on him. In daily use, a wallet such as this would have held paper money, credit cards, and irreplaceable family photographs, all of which staffers have employed appropriately or thrown into a convenient dumpster as part of the curatorial process.

Interactive Exhibit: In this display, museumgoers are invited to put on headphones and listen to us having a hearty laugh at your expense. The first "ha-ha-ha" you hear belongs to Adrian Ffoulks, the director of the museum, who allows himself a rare but heartfelt chuckle. The subsequent belly laughs are from our board of trustees, who appreciate the comedy of watching you try to get any of "your" possessions back (good luck!), followed by a paroxysm of hilarity from the throats of our amply funded legal department. We hope you have enjoyed your visit. Now run along.

Take My Globalist Wife

Two globalists are walking down the street. They're hungry, because of the patriotic tariff on foreign foods, and they're trying to find a way to get some money. They pass a First Baptist Pentecostal Non-Globalist Church of the Redeemer, and they see a big sign: CONVERT TO OUR FAITH AND WE WILL PAY YOU $100 CASH. The first globalist says to the second globalist, "Oh, I could never do that. They don't believe in globalism." The second globalist says, "Well, that's fine for you to say, but I could sure use that hundred bucks." So he goes in, and the first globalist waits for him on the sidewalk, and after a while the second globalist comes out. The first globalist asks him, "So, how did it go? Did you get the money?" The second globalist looks at him and says, "Is that all you globalists ever think about?"

∗∗∗

A Catholic priest, a Buddhist monk, and a globalist former presidential adviser are in a lifeboat. The Catholic priest says, "Let us all pray together to our divine Father, and a ship will come along and rescue us." The Buddhist monk says, "Let us all meditate together on the sublime Buddha's embodiment of the oneness of all being, and a ship will come along and rescue us." And the globalist former presidential adviser says, "I don't know about you guys, but I'm returning to my previous job at Goldman Sachs!"

✳✳✳

A globalist goes to work for his father-in-law, who happens to be a non-globalist, and, after he's been working for him for about a year, the globalist arrives at the office and discovers that his special VIP parking permit has been canceled. So the globalist goes to his father-in-law and asks him, "Why was my special VIP parking permit canceled? Does the fact that I'm a globalist have anything to do with it?" The father-in-law stares at him for a long time. Then he says, "Of course not! I have some very, very close friends who are globalists."

✳✳✳

A globalist economist is sitting in his shop on the Lower East Side, making international trade agreements, when a customer comes in very upset and says, "I have a complaint about this international trade agreement you made for me." The globalist economist looks up from his international-trade-agreement-making bench, adjusts his spectacles, and says, "Come back Monday, when I will be at Davos."

✳✳✳

A globalist mother and her son are at the beach. The son goes in for a swim, and suddenly he starts to drown. The globalist mother screams, "Save my boy! Save my boy!" A lifeguard jumps in, battles the powerful riptides, and almost drowns himself. After a terrific struggle, he saves the son, and he carries him to the globalist mother. She looks at her son and says to the lifeguard, "He had a hat." So the globalist mother and her son sue the lifeguard and win a huge settlement from an ultra-liberal proactive globalist judge at the World Court, in The Hague.

**

A representative of the Deep State is handing out leaflets on a corner in the garment district. He stops a man and says, "Excuse me, sir, are you a globalist?" The man replies, "I'm a furrier." The representative of the Deep State says, "Yes, but are you a globalist?" The furrier becomes angry and shouts at him, "Numbskull, I told you I'm a furrier! When did you ever meet a furrier who *wasn't* a globalist?"

**

A young globalist woman and a young cosmopolite man fall in love and decide to get married. The parents of the globalist woman want to meet the parents of the cosmopolite groom, so they all go out to dinner, and the parents of the globalist woman ask the cosmopolite parents, "And how do you want our grandchildren to be raised—as globalists or as cosmopolites?" There is a long silence. Finally, the waiter, who has overheard the conversation, interrupts: "Forgive me for putting in my two cents, and please excuse my ignorance, but aren't globalists and cosmopolites pretty much the same thing?"

＊＊＊

My globalist mother-in-law is so unpatriotic. She says to me, "Do you want to be an internationalist citizen of the world? Or do you want to spend the rest of your life sitting in your Buick in Mamaroneck?" And talk about elitist! My globalist mother-in-law is so elitist, she plays mah-jongg with Kristalina Georgieva, the CEO of the World Bank! And out of touch with the real America? You gotta be kidding me! My globalist mother-in-law is so out of touch with the real America that, when I tell her I'm going to Pocatello, Idaho, on a business trip, she says, "Pocatello? You mean the Italian handbag designer?" Don't get me started.

＊＊＊

Take my globalist wife—please! Or, for the strict globalists who speak only Esperanto: *Prenu mian tutmondisman edzinon—bonvole!*

It's the Data, Dolts

> The whistle-blower Christopher Wylie held a roomful of British lawmakers rapt for three and a half hours on Tuesday, like a pink-haired, nose-ringed oracle sent from the future to explain data . . .
>
> At times, he seemed slightly pitying of British officials who are investigating data-mining, saying they did not have enough resources and lacked "a robust technical background."
>
> "I have had to explain and re-explain and re-explain and re-explain, you know, how relational databases work, what is an eigenvector, what is dimensionality reduction," he said.
>
> —"Cambridge Analytica Whistle-Blower Contends Data-Mining Swung Brexit Vote," in *The New York Times*

Explanation No. 1:

I will try to go slowly, so I don't lose anybody. I've talked about relational databases already, but if you need a refresher please go to http://relationaldb.@^+66–7777.fda .lihgiw. Next, I will explain eigenvectors. These are just vectors, and we all know what vectors are—they're things that go someplace, right? So you take regular vectors and make them eigen, and you get eigenvectors. Now let's tackle dimensionality reduction. That simply means that you take a certain dimensionality and then you reduce it. So—are we good? Good!

Explanation No. 2:

Apparently, some of you with less robust tech backgrounds did not completely follow me the first time, so let's review. Relational databases—I mean, come on, how hard can that be? They're databases that relate to one another. Use your heads. Now, eigenvectors—we all use eigenvectors in everyday life, they're practically self-explanatory. You take an ordinary vector and simply "eigen" it—please. Dimensionality reduction is so easy I'm not even going to explain it this time. Look at the diagram and work it out for yourselves.

Explanation No. 3:

I can't believe you are eminent British lawmakers and yet can't seem to grasp such basic stuff. Bring me my whiteboard. Okay, from the top, once again—relational databases are so ridiculously easy that even a two-year-old can understand them, and, in fact, many actual two-year-olds do understand them and are working for our company right now, making great big lovely heaps of money mining data and swinging elections, all while still in their nappies! Simply put, a relational database is a database that's related either to another database or to Camilla Parker Bowles. (No, I'm *kidding*, guys.)

And why in the world can't you understand eigenvectors? Look back over what I said in my first explanation. What do you mean, you weren't taking notes? Do you think I'm telling you all this just to hear myself talk?

I want all of you to put your hands out on your desks. Yes, right now. You, too, Mr. Chief Solicitor! Now I'm going to rap you all on the knuckles with my phone. Yes, of course it hurts! It's supposed to hurt. If it doesn't hurt, you won't remember. I advise you all to take notes the next time.

I'm doing some deep breathing before I proceed to dimensionality reduction, iteration three. Okay, let me give you an example that I'm sure will be obvious even to brilliant Solons of the bar like yourselves. Have you ever been to a 3D movie? I'm sure your mommies and daddies took you when you were little. Remember you wore those funny glasses? Well, the "D" stands for "dimension." Now, if we want to reduce the dimensionality, we simply take the glasses off. And what dimensionality do we see the movie in then? Two-dimensionality! Very good. That is what we mean by dimensionality reduction, and exactly the same principle applies to these very large computers you seem to have absolutely no clue about.

Explanation No. 4:

I've had it up to *here* with you people! I believe you actually know less than you did when we began. Somehow, everything I've tried to teach you has only made you stupider. I am sad, and ashamed, and very, very disappointed in you. Do I need visual aids? Must I dress up as an eigenvector? Must I bake relational-database cupcakes? What is wrong with you? Deep down, do you not *want* to know what a relational database is? Is the problem cultural? Is it my nose ring? Would you understand better if I took my nose ring out? What if I put some extra nose rings in? I am at my wit's end. Wait—what if *you* put in nose rings?

The Next Day:

Wonderful! You all look splendid, and I've gone over the quizzes I gave you, post–nose rings, and you got every question right. So that was the problem all along—the nose rings! Now, if you want to become really clever, we'll do the hair.

Ask the Compliance Expert

Q: I am pursuing due diligence regarding the accepted best practices having to do with theft. When I'm stealing packages from my neighbor's porch, how do I remain fully compliant and not go outside the bounds of the law?

A: Let me answer your question with a question: Have you been caught? If not, for all practical purposes you are in compliance.

Q: While dumping toxic substances into the reservoir, I suddenly wondered whether there might be some old laws on the books that I should comply with. Are there?

A: No, not to my immediate knowledge—or yours.

Q: I am interested in making millions of Americans addicted to the drugs that my company sells. This is okay from a compliance standpoint, right?

A: Absolutely! I would not be a registered expert in compliance if I told you otherwise. Indeed, I am surprised at the tone of uncertainty in your question. As a compliance issue, selling drugs and making people addicted to them is itself complying with a higher law, covered by the ancient Roman formula *lex quodquod cupio* ("the law [is] whatever I want"). One must look inside oneself and ask, "Is this what I want?" If the answer is "Yes, it is!" then that's the law, and the relevant compliance obligations have been met.

Q: I recently discovered that for many years I have unwittingly complied with laws against punching passersby in the face on the street. Who even knew that such laws existed? But I complied with them all the same! Now, because of a change in personal feelings, I would like not to comply with these laws anymore. Can I get some free punches on credit for all the punches that I didn't throw in the past (such as at the guy last week in Times Square)?

A: Believe me, I know how frustrating it is to find that you have accidentally complied when noncompliance was an option that would have made you feel much better. Complying with not punching people in the face, in practice, is voluntary and self-enforcing. In other words, no one is a better judge of when to punch and when not to punch than you are. None of these rules are written in stone. If you feel like it, by all means, punch away. We compliance experts can work something out later.

Q: A chemical that I made at my factory and then intentionally released in a neighborhood of people I don't like had the result of killing hundreds of my possible enemies and also many non-enemy bystanders. Now I am told that some tricky compliance issues need to be sorted out. How long will that take, and is it permissible to delete the emails that various police officials, attorneys, and survivors keep sending me?

A: One of the thorniest compliance areas that we have to deal with is murder. Again, it's a matter of interpretation, but when you cause another person's death, your act may fall into the category of murder, or, to use a courtroom term, "homicide." Do not let these weighted words intimidate you, however. They serve mainly as placeholders while we look more closely at readjusting the compliance structure to your particular situation. Say that you are being asked to comply with prison time or even some lethal-injection exposure as a result of your having "murdered" X or Y individual(s). That demand goes both ways, because you can also require the individuals imposing such penalties to comply with your executing them as well. Can they comply with chemicals entering the AC units of their apartments or houses and poisoning them in their sleep? "Comply with *this*!" you shout. Compliance will always be a two-way street.

Q: It seems like I comply and comply and comply again, and it's never enough. Will there be no end to this complying? I frequently commit acts that are then crime-shamed as being "against the law," "just plain wrong," or even "sociopathic." Is that fair? Can you help me?

A: Help you? I *am* you, and I say "Go for it!" In the end, only we can judge.

Italy

One of my lifelong ambitions is never to go to Italy. When I was a boy, in Ohio, my parents urged me to wish for something more realistic, such as never going anywhere in Missouri (several states away). Mom and Dad knew that never going to Italy would be unattainable for people like us. But I kept dreaming, as I pored over my lists of places in Italy I dreaded to see, foods I hoped not to eat, and famous cathedrals I did not want to go on tours of. After all, a big part of the fun of never traveling somewhere is in the planning. My folks had the wisdom to allow me that, though they knew the disappointment sure to come.

My own inborn artistic temperament created an additional problem, because I happen to be highly susceptible to the visual arts. Much as I try to scrub my brain of all knowledge of painting and sculpture, I can't. With great effort, I got rid of every word in the art lover's vocabulary except for one pesky holdout: "provenance." Even today, if I find myself at a cocktail party and a particular work of art comes up in conversation, out of my mouth always leaps the question "Yes, but what is its provenance?" As it turns out, "provenance" is the only word you need in order to fall into a bottomless pit of art-related discussion that always seems to lead to Italy (usually by way of Vasari). For me, in this direction lies madness.

I also have a strange and regrettable weakness for inventing catchy acronyms for art museums. Even if I firmly resolve to use a museum's entire name whenever that museum comes up, my natural bent betrays me. For example, I faithfully try to say the "Museum of Modern Art," but what I blurt out instead is "MoMA" (an acronym I invented some years ago). Similarly, I always want to refer to the Los Angeles County Museum of Art by its full name, and never say "LACMA," the popular acronym I came up with (though it is, I admit, much shorter and handier). And not many people know that I'm the person who thought of calling the famous Musée du Louvre, in Paris, "MUDULOU" (pronounced "moo-doo-loo"). In these now widely adopted coinages of mine, I discern a vague, threatening specter somehow inexorably drawing me toward Italy—and I tremble.

I had a close call the other day. I was on an airplane that was diverted from Heathrow to Italy, because of bad weather. Now, I consider Heathrow my second home. As a citizen of the world (except for Italy), I would have preferred that the flight brave the storm so that I could relax in Heathrow's Citizens of the World (Except for Italy) VIP Lounge. But the pilot of the plane was the rugged type who looks like a male model and therefore seeks the male model's natural habitat—i.e., Italy. The plane kept on going, Italy bound, while I sweated in my seat. The dream of a lifetime was about to come to an inglorious end. Then, ten minutes before we entered Italian airspace, the weather over London cleared and the plane turned around. My dream still lived! I began to weep quietly. I told myself, "Hold on to your dreams! You will never go to Italy, if only you believe you won't!"

This near-Italy experience has only made me more determined. Never going to Italy might take a lot of sloth, but I believe I am up to it. First, I'll need to be in the very worst physical condition. That way, when someone interrogates me about why I haven't yet gone to Italy, I'll answer, "Can't! Too out of shape!" Second, I'll have to write a book exposing organized crime in every major Italian city. Then the Italian government will not allow me to cross the border, because of the potential costs of heightened police protection. And, third, I'll lose my passport! The beauty of that strategy is in its simplicity. I'm surprised I've never thought of it before.

I can hear the Italy-goers, in their multitudes, telling me that I'm only cheating myself. But look at it this way: I'm also not carrying around a small flag, leading a tour group into one basilica or another and bumping into you as you try to get a better look at that gorgeous-whatever Vasari. In the busiest Italian places, check out the one less-crowded corner. The person helpfully not standing there is me.

In Billionaires Is the Preservation
of the World

Billionaires are all around us, but do we ever stop and notice them? We pass through their habitats and provide them the tax nourishment that biologists say is necessary for their survival. But simply increasing their wealth is not the same as understanding the importance of even a single-digit billionaire in the complex web of life. Take a moment and examine a video of a billionaire. Seen from up close, the delicate striations on the belly of Secretary of the Treasury Steven Mnuchin (to pick one example) reveal mini-universes. Nature, wearing its hat as the free market, has made him, and every billionaire, unique.

Observing billionaires in situ takes patience. Only a few of us will ever get to watch a billionaire feeding. If you are lucky enough to see a billionaire behind his enormous desk masticating his eccentric diet of choice while you sit quietly in front of him, hungry and unfed—a condition the billionaire seems to require in order to accept your presence—you will have four minutes to make your pitch. Avoid sudden movements that might startle the billionaire, for if that happens he will signal to the others and they will hurry off shrieking through the penthouse canopy. Billionaires are notoriously shy and often take on an ordinary appearance to escape detection, even masking themselves in khaki such as anybody might wear. Thus the observer must exert extra caution in identifying them.

Formerly, billionaires were so plentiful in western trout streams that, it was said, you could walk from bank to bank on their hats and never wet your feet. And once, historians claim, the endless flights of billionaires darkened the skies above Long Island until their cackling drowned out ordinary conversation. Fortunately, those bygone days are still here. Thanks to increased public awareness, billionaires remain plentiful and provide a vital resource. Today, the fate of global ecosystems often depends on nature's own life preserver, the billionaire.

Here is how the healing process works. Say you are a nonprofit out to save the oceans. First, you find a billionaire. Using due diligence, you search out exactly the right billionaire—one who, as you discover, loves netsuke. To help nature along, you get some netsuke and put it on a trail where the billionaire is likely to jog by. Soon the billionaire appears; he sniffs the netsuke, and absorbs it into his private collection. Then, and only then, do you emerge from the brush to tell him about your deep and long-held admiration for him. From this point your presentation is carried out carefully, until, suddenly, the plight of the oceans clicks with the billionaire! Now that crucial part of the planet can be saved.

Certain billionaires have evolved traits specially adapted to saving rain forests. Others have inherited characteristics well suited for preserving woodlands and open spaces near their multi-thousand-square-foot fourth homes. A particular kind of billionaire has developed extra financial digits ideal for making beachfront dunes off-limits to out-of-towners. Some billionaires' adaptations seem to serve decorative purposes only, or their conservation functions have yet to be discovered. It is up to us to discover them. Any billionaire left untapped equals a part of the earth that will consequently die.

We have all read about Croesus, the highest-wealth individual of classical times, and how his underwriting of the process of plant photosynthesis provided for the generous production of atmospheric oxygen that we still enjoy today. But the people of Croesus's own time took him for granted, as we do too often with billionaires. They do not have to save anything if they don't want to. Only if we cultivate them will they fulfill the functions that nature has designed them to perform. For each of us, that means being nice to them, paying attention to their needs, and never speaking of them in such demeaning or out-of-date terms as "capitalist swine." They are no more swine than we are, merely very different human beings with a particular role to fill in making the planet able to support life. Our job is to draw them out and give them comfort. Is that too much to ask?

Consider what is at stake:

We now face an existential challenge to the planet in global warming. Fixing this problem will be beyond the power of any one billionaire. It might take three of them, or even four. But the question is: Which four? With life itself depending on it, how do we determine which billionaires to kiss up to? This is where our knowledge of billionaires—our "billionaire-ology"—will have to be improved. A massive group effort will be called for. Every one of us, from university presidents to museum heads to caterers to legislators to florists, will have to get together and pool what we have learned, by hard, boots-on-the-ground-at-the-gala-benefit experience, about our valuable friends, the billionaires.

Creative

For many years, I have taught creative writing. I am licensed by the state to teach it at all levels: Beginning Creative (BC), Moderately Creative (MC), and Extremely Creative (EC). That last and highest level is actually subdivided into three other levels: Pulitzer, Man/Woman Booker, and Nobel, which is the highest of all creative-writing levels, and which very few students reach. In fact, some of my students choose voluntarily not to try for that level, although, technically speaking, they probably could handle it. Creativity is the goal, but we are aware that it is possible to get *too* creative.

When I say these students could handle it, what I mean is that they have the chops. The writing chops, that is. Civilians may not know what I'm referring to when I use that term. They may not even know that they are civilians. But civilians are what we call them, because we are also in the military—the creative-writing military—and our weapons are words.

People say you can't teach creativity. Well, I am living proof that you can. As I once told Harold Pinter, creativity is like a third arm, and my job is to help you free it. He ran off screaming, and that became his first play, which, unfortunately, was never produced but caused quite a stir when it was workshopped. Pinter was a very bright kid, and extremely, *extremely* creative. I cannot emphasize too strongly how creative Hal Pinter was. In fact, he placed out of Beginning Creative and into Extremely Creative two days after he showed up here. It seemed that all my students back then—I'm talking the mid-fifties—were very sharp and already knew a lot when they came to me.

That is a far cry from today. Now I get a lot of students who are just plain stupid. We're not supposed to say that, because we want to keep up the number of kids who apply to the program. But it's just a simple fact. Some of the kids I have in my classes know absolutely nothing. Mention a book like *Who Moved My Cheese?* and they've never heard of it. I mean, like . . . hello? How can a supposedly educated person not have heard of that book? The other day in class I said that something one of the kids wrote was in the style of Jacqueline Susann. I got nothing but blank looks. I said, "Susann, Jackie Susann! Wrote *Valley of the Dolls*, for heaven's sake! Used to go on *The Tonight Show* with Johnny Carson!" They had never heard of Johnny Carson, either. Such ignorance almost makes me give up.

Creative-writing teachers have affairs with two kinds of people: other creative-writing teachers, and creative-writing students. Personally—and I know this will get me in trouble—I prefer students. Why? Because, generally speaking, they are hotter.

Sorry. I apologize for the preceding paragraph. I was just kidding. That's an example of what I was saying about getting too creative. Like my famous short story about the affair that a disguised version of myself had with Jackie Susann. In fact, the affair never occurred. I made it up, using my creative imagination combined with critical thinking.

That combination is a secret technique of mine, but if you want to learn more about it you'll have to take my course. I got in trouble for that short story, too, because I doused it with gasoline, set it on fire, and threw it onto somebody's porch, burning down the entire house.

Writers have always been persecuted for their work. That is truer of creative writers, and truest of creative-writing teachers. All writing has consequences, just as I was persecuted for the consequences of that short story. I have never let being jailed for arson silence me, but have continued to teach in what is called a low-residency program, which means I can teach from prison. For this purpose, Zoom is great. My students don't know where I am, though they have asked why I am apparently wearing an orange jumpsuit and picking up trash along the highway during class.

Creative writing matters because the human species is hardwired for narrative. In caveman days, we sat around our fires and spun stories, just as creative-writing students today sit around seminar tables and play video games. Recently, I had the uncanny experience of regressing to one of my former selves—a caveman. There was the old campfire. Another caveman walked into the circle of light and proceeded to hold me and my fellow cave people rapt with narrative. However, I quickly stopped him. I said I thought he should interrogate the beginning of that narrative, the part with the ice bear. He left the circle of light, came back, and began again, skipping the ice-bear part. All of us sitting around the fire agreed that the narrative worked better and was much clearer without the ice bear.

And so the first creative-writing class was born.

Once and Future Prince

> The seven-time Grammy Award winner reportedly
> left behind a vault containing so much music his
> estate could put out an album a year for the next
> century.
>
> —ABC News

2025. Wildfires again sweep the West Coast. Windstorms bearing sand and ash cause mass evacuations in Southern California. Title track from Prince's latest album, *Rain of Colors Other Than Purple*, reaches No. 17 on *Billboard*'s Top Forty.

2043. Last remaining Antarctic ice shelf slides into the ocean, leading to an additional two meters in sea-level rise and total inundation of lower Manhattan. *Prince 2 Infinity*, released in time to qualify for the 2043 awards season, wins Best New Secret-Vault Album of the Year.

2052. Canada, accepting the inevitable, cedes the lower half of its territory to migrant caravans from the United States. Prince's single "Love EvN Sexier" becomes migrants' unofficial anthem.

2055. Nunavut, the Native nation above the Arctic Circle, begins construction of forty-foot-high steel wall. Publicity for the double-album set *Piece O' Prince* generates international buzz.

2064. Carbon-capture technology finally begins to make dent in atmospheric carbon dioxide. No Prince album released because of dispute among heirs.

2065. Carbon-capture technology purchased by Exxon-Mobil, mothballed. Heirs resolve dispute. *U R Prince* gets respectable numbers on Arctic-Antarctic Spotify.

2069. Aliens land super-air-conditioned spaceship on last remaining part of New Mexico desert still above water. X6y2 Craniums, alien High Commander, reveals that Prince's newest, *AstroMusiKology*, is a personal favorite.

2071. Final melting of tundra leads to flooding of Central Asia and displacement of millions. Discovery of previously unknown Prince symbol in a secret drawer requires redesign of *Raspberry Hazmat Beret* CD cover.

2072. Aliens announce that they believe strongly in Earth's future, plan to stay and open Prince-themed water park and cyclotron.

2073. Last tuna salad sandwich on planet is eaten by coal industry lobbyist in Winnipeg, new U.S. capital. Realistic hologram of Prince accepts Post-Lifetime Achievement Award at Rock and Roll Climate-Controlled Deep-Underground Survival Bunker of Fame.

2076. Typhoons bury Japan in plastic from the Greater Pacific Gyre (former Pacific Ocean). Hundreds of Prince impersonators perform his "Hot E-Nuff 4 U??" at Super Bowl CIX, in Gander, Newfoundland, USA.

2077. Citing "impossible" weather, aliens leave, causing loss of confidence in global markets, financial panic. Release of Prince's updated greatest hits album postponed.

2083. Mass extinctions, desertification of Europe, nuclear war. Critical opinion of Prince's newest, *Little Red Sustainable Electric-Powered Self-Driving Corvette*, questions album's faithfulness to his original vision.

2085–86. Warmest nuclear winter ever recorded in Northern Hemisphere. Prince's special *Dark 'N' Ashy* Christmas album falls flat.

2097. Human race facing extinction. Carbon-dioxide-breathing bots discover Prince, start their own Prince fan site.

0. Carbon-dioxide-breathing bots discard old calendar, establish binary calendar beginning at zero. Bot-produced album of outtakes, *Prince +–==–+*, results in five hundred million bot downloads.

1. Flush with cash, bot-owned record company builds huge monuments to Prince in non-spatial dimensions.

10. Anti-bots from black-hole galaxy invade planet formerly known as Earth, make peace with resident bots through mutual love of Prince.

100. Fungus brought by anti-bots begins to wipe out Earth bots. Fungus found in ordinary bathroom grouting ravages anti-bots. Surviving bots and anti-bots unite to wire entire planet into single intercontinental cold-fusion-powered sound system to play Prince.

110. Last remaining human Prince fan is honored by bots and then ritually dematerialized. Global sound system plays AI-generated Prince mixtapes around the clock, commercial-free.

111. Bot archeologists discover hidden trove of unreleased Billy Ray Cyrus music. Bot mass suicides depopulate planet.

11011. =+==#=+=#*Prince Farewell Album*+-=-=+ becomes a megahit on several planets of Alpha Centauri. New visitations of aliens land in former Minneapolis, initiate dune-buggy-and-bathysphere tours of important sites in career of Prince.

11111. Unblinking eye of God appears in heavens; the other eye and facial features resemble Prince's.

Infinity sign. Alpha and Omega, the End of Time. Prince goes on forever.

Etymology of Some Common Typos

The word "typo" is actually a misnomer. Derived from a phrase that denotes error, it suggests that the typist has made a mistake. In fact, what we call typos are more accurately described as variations. Take "anmd," which often appears when we think we have typed the conjunction "and." In some parts of the Anglophone world, both versions of this word—"and" and "anmd" (or "and" anmd "anmd")—are acceptable, just as the mistyped "trhe" may be used interchangeably with the (or trhe) more conventional article "the." Of course, there are exceptions, or erxceptions, such as the word "erxceptions" itself, which is also accepted but considered impolite.

"Anmd" and "trhe," unlike "erxception," both derive from ancient oral tradition. In Old, Old Norse, the stray "m" and "r" are believed to have corrupted "and" and "the" in common speech through the negligence or haste of slob members of the ur-Norse community. When monks transcribed these words directly from the mouths of the speakers, they became grossed out, but dutifully included the variations on their stain-spattered vellum manuscripts, and, as such, these so-called typos have been handed down.

Variations sometimes occur as typographic representations of consonants that seem to have migrated sideways in the mouth. This is the case with variations containing the letter "p," such as "yopu" ("you"). As Indo-European peoples moved laterally in their wanderings, west to east (or vice versa), the plosive consonants did something similar on the tongue. Thus, we may be typing along and see an unfamiliar sentence, such as "I will be goping home," appear on the screen. Unconsciously, we have typed exactly what an ancient Indo-European person would have said. The sentence "Dopn't dop that" (in everyday modern English, "Don't do that") has been seen spelled out in finger paint on the walls of the limestone caves of Lascaux, France, where human occupation dates to more than 30,000 BCE. Moreover, in certain contexts the second-person singular "yopu" appears to have been not a pronoun but the proper name of a particular cave individual, and ideally should be capitalized, as "Yopu."

What do we know of this Yopu, or of any of the Indo-Europeans? Here is where our "typos" may be trying to tell us something. When these ancient humans used aspirated consonants, such as "h" (or the "wh" sound), our mistypings show that they often snuck in a seemingly gratuitous "j," as in "whjat" ("what"), "hjere" ("here"), or "hjog" ("hog"). An ancient Indo-European sentence such as "Whjat is thjat hjog doping hjere?" makes sense only if we posit that the speaker was trying to come off as Swedish. Why he or she would want to do that is another question, but it does shed light on a weird kind of insecurity that permeated the society. The faster we type, the more intriguing this window into the distant past becomes. "Trhe quiclk brownb fsocx jumptde over rtha laxy dopg," a typing-practice sentence that all of us learned in high school, includes, in this typed-super-fast version, at least eight different proto-language families struggling to be reborn.

Modern humans who type "fsocx" for "fox" likely have some Neanderthal DNA. Perhaps the well-known practice sentence describes an encounter that occurred regularly between Ice Age foxes and Neanderthal dogs. Bone-density studies of canine skeletons found in conjunction with Neanderthal shell middens indicate high concentrations of gene pairings often associated with laziness—for what that's worth. The word "jumptde" is an elongated verb form of pre-Celtic origin, later common in Turkic languages, which fell out of favor when it became kind of a pain. And, remarkably, "over" is one of those rare words that are exactly the same in every language, extinct or living, around the world.

Nopw we fast-foprward top trhe technop era, amnd trhe influence opf Autopcoprrect. (Or, "Nope we fast-foppish tomorrow trh technophobe era, amid tre influence old Autocorrect.") Today, corrections that used to take weeks happen automatically. But here a darker process seems to be goping on. When we set out to create a text message, the echoes of lost languages, and all connections to our shared human past, are erased. Text a harmless sentence like "I'm here, ready to help," and whjat may pop up is "I'm here, ready to Hal." Huh? Who is this "Hal"? We will never know, nor will the text's no doubt baffled recipient. If, instead of "Hal," the name supplied had been "Hjal," we would have met another shadowy figure from the mists of time, someone who might conceivably have known Yopu. But, thanks to Autocorrect, poor Hjal is long forgotten. Type in his name, and it will be corrected to "Hal," just another ordinary present-day guy, and we are the poorer for it.

In the Mail

JANUARY 8

Dear Sir,

Your check has been cut and is ready to be mailed to you. The person who will mail it to you is currently being mailed to us. We will keep a close eye on our mail, and as soon as it arrives, with him in it, we will transfer the check to him to mail to you immediately.

FEBRUARY 15

Dear Sir,

Thank you for your inquiry. Your check is still here, ready to go, but the person who was mailed to us so that he could mail it to you took longer than expected to be mailed. When he finally did arrive, with the rest of our mail, he was mistaken for junk mail and ended up in the recycled mail. We have put in a special request, and another person who will promptly mail your check to you is being mailed to us, via overnight mail.

MARCH 11

Dear Sir,

The person who was being mailed to us by overnight mail so that he could mail your check to you was mailed from someplace north of the Arctic Circle (we are told), where night lasts a long time, which naturally affects the mail. We are closely tracking this overnight mailing and expect it to arrive at our offices with our other mail as soon as night up there is over—no later than mid-April, we believe. Please be assured that your check is sitting right here on our desk, still crisp and fresh and beautiful, all set to be mailed.

MARCH 23

Dear Sir,

Just to reassure you that your check really does exist, we are looking at it right now: it is eight inches long by three and a half inches high, printed on that handsome mini-herringbone-patterned background that the best checks are printed on, and it says "Pay to the order of," followed by your clearly typed and correctly spelled name. So, there can be no mistake about the exact person for whom the check is intended—you. Your address also appears on the check, which will come in handy when the check is mailed.

MARCH 24

Dear Sir,

Apologies for contacting you again so soon after our previous communication about your check, but we admired it again this morning, here on our desk, and somehow, in our absence, the sum seems to have been changed to a larger number than it was yesterday! It really is a substantial check. You must be very eager to have such a check mailed to you, and, indeed, in all likelihood, it probably will be mailed before long.

APRIL 12

Dear Sir,

The mail containing the person whose job it was to mail your check to you arrived, and he has mailed you your check. Unfortunately, our mail service uses a mail drop in which there are two regular-mail slots for outgoing mail, the first marked EARTH MAIL and the second marked OTHER. Assuming that the EARTH MAIL slot had something to do with Earth Day, and thinking that was not appropriate, he dropped your check into the slot marked OTHER. A reasonable mistake—but, regrettably, the OTHER slot is for mail addressed to places other than Earth. This may cause a further mail delay, for which we apologize.

NOVEMBER 18

Dear Sir,

We met a fellow in the past two to three weeks who said that he ran into your check at the famous *Star Wars* bar sometime last summer, although he forgets the exact date. We just thought you would like to know.

DECEMBER 1

Dear Sir,

Yes, we suppose we could put a "stop" on your check and issue (but not mail) a check to replace the check that we weren't mailing previously—but, really, why bother?

DECEMBER 8

Dear Sir,

Against our better judgment, we have voided your original check and issued a replacement. Oh, what a gorgeous thing this spanking new check is! At the moment, it is sitting, pert and pretty, on our desk, waiting to be mailed.

FEBRUARY 9

Dear Sir,

We were getting way too attached to each other, your check and us, and so we made the painful decision to end the relationship. The check has just been mailed via Ever Go ground service, and we are monitoring its progress. Already, it has traveled half the distance to you, and we are informed that very soon it will cover half the remaining distance, and then, quickly, half the remaining distance after that, etc. So be on the lookout!

FEBRUARY 11

Dear Sir,

The driver of the Ever Go truck informs us that he is one-thirty-second of an inch from your address and expects to be one-sixty-fourth of an inch from it shortly. He will make the delivery sometime between eight o'clock Eastern Standard Time this morning (Tuesday, 2/11) and infinity. We appreciate your patience.

Dracula Is off the Case

Come in, Dracula. Have a seat. Can I get you a cup of joe? Oh, I forgot—Joe's not here. He's working days now. Would you settle for some coffee? Okay, suit yourself.

I called you in because we need to talk. You know how highly I value you. Just between us, you're the best detective I've got. Joe is good, but (also between us) he has not been in top form lately. He's pale, weak, and drained. In fact, the whole department is pale, weak, and drained. I know you've been taking up the slack for everybody, and yet every day you seem to get stronger and grow more into the job. Your work has been irreproachable. I don't know how you come up with some of your leads. What, do you change into a bat and fly around and go into people's apartments through their open windows or skylights? You're amazing.

Your performance is not the problem. It's your emotions. You get too involved, you're too committed to your work, if that makes any sense. And you ride the other officers pretty hard—I mean, you climb right up on them, hook the toes of your strange, pointy shoes in their belts, put your cape over them, even give them hickies when you become upset. I appreciate your passion, but that's just not professional deportment, and I can't allow it.

So, for the time being, I am moving you to desk duty. I'm taking you off every case you're working on, as of tonight, which, as I see out the station house window, is the full moon. I'm ordering you to turn in your cape with the huge collar, and that weird medallion or whatever it is you wear on a chain around your neck, and I'm also going to need that box of dirt you sleep in. And your gun. You will get them all back, don't worry. This is just a temporary reassignment, so that you can clear your head—under that hairdo you apparently drew on with Magic Marker—and come to terms with some of your personal issues. Don't think you're being given a make-work job, either. Your English is pretty good, if not totally there yet, and you are the only native Transylvanian speaker on the entire force. There may be documents for you to translate, and you'll be on call as an interpreter, should the need arise.

I anticipated that you might want to file a grievance, and—can I give you a tip about that? The Grievance office is at headquarters, you have to file in person, and it's not open at night. Grievance closes at four in the afternoon, I believe. And as I understand it, that is not an optimum time for you. We've given you flexible hours here, and it's worked out. Most police officers tend not to like that one-hour-after-sunset-to-one-hour-before-sunrise shift, and I know you love it, so I've broken some regs to accommodate you and let you write your own ticket, basically. If you go to Grievance, you would endanger that, plus you'd risk turning into a pumpkin or whatever you think might happen to you if you're ever out in daylight. So I would advise you to very carefully consider any decision to go to Grievance.

I understand how you might be feeling right now. You know, I wasn't always a precinct captain. Believe it or not,

I was once a rookie like yourself, a little green around the edges. You probably noticed I have a couple of bolts coming out of my head. And did I ever show you this? That's right—both my hands are sewn on. Same with my feet, my legs, everything. If you can keep a secret, my birth name was not O'Hara. In fact, I wasn't even born; I was built in a guy's basement. The wingnut who made me—no disrespect intended—gave me his own last name, which I changed to O'Hara when I reached legal age. And years ago, my first boss, Captain Mickey Wolfman, God rest his soul, did the exact same thing to me that I'm doing to you.

I'll never forget it. One day, Captain Wolfman took me aside, put his big, hairy paw on my shoulder, and said he was sending me to the impound lot to write down engine IDs from confiscated vehicles until I could actually talk. Back then, everything I said came out as a kind of preverbal "*uuhhnnnh.*" Captain Wolfman was absolutely right to make that move, and obviously I did eventually pick up regular human speech. I hated the old bastard's guts at the time, but today I thank him with all my heart. Maybe someday you'll feel the same about me. Now get the hell out of my office, Dracula, and let me go back to work.

Two Plus Two

Alabama: 5

Alaska: Leaning 4

Arizona: T.B.D.

Arkansas: 3-something

California: 4.000001

Colorado: About 4?

Connecticut: $4.4 billion

Delaware: Ordinary 4

Florida: Commonsense 5

Georgia: 11,776 to go

Hawaii: 4-point-oh

Idaho: .40 cal.

Illinois: Make offer.

Indiana: Ask again later.

Iowa: 2,024

Kansas: 4/not 4

Kentucky: Nonnegotiable 5

Louisiana: Boo-coo 3

Maine: 5 but looking

Maryland: 4 and holding

Massachusetts: As 4 as it gets

Michigan: Crossed-out-tattoo 4

Minnesota: 4, if that's okay?

Mississippi: 6 and falling

Missouri: 3, 4, or 5—give or take

Montana: At least 5

Nebraska: 5-ish 4

Nevada: 3, and the over

New Hampshire: 4 for now

New Jersey: 5, and the under

New Mexico: 5, please

New York: "5?" Please.

North Carolina: Turning 4

North Dakota: 5 below

Ohio: The 4 that is a 5

Oklahoma: Never 4

Oregon: 3.999999

Pennsylvania: "n" = the Unknown

Rhode Island: Fried calamari!

South Carolina: Future 4

South Dakota: Tentative 7

Tennessee: Trending 3

Texas: 5 lone stars

Utah: Computers down

Vermont: Nonnegotiable 4

Virginia: 4, né 5

Washington: Fine with 4

West Virginia: Damn sure 6

Wisconsin: Conflicted 4

Wyoming: 4 the hard way